ELEMENTS OF W

# Sharpening Turning Tools

Selected Readings from *American Woodturner*, journal of the American Association of Woodturners

AAW | AMERICAN ASSOCIATION OF WOODTURNERS

American Association of Woodturners | 222 Landmark Center, 75 Fifth Street West, St. Paul, MN 55102-7704
877-595-9094 | www.woodturner.org

# Contents

Published by American Association of Woodturners,
222 Landmark Center, 75 5th St. W., St. Paul, MN 55102-7704.
877-595-9094, www.woodturner.org.





*American Woodturner* (ISSN 0895-9005) is published bimonthly by American Association of Woodturners.

*Sharpening Turning Tools*
ISBN: 978-1-939662-15-6

Printed on Demand in United States of America
American Association of Woodturners, www.woodturner.org

# Introduction

It's often said that a woodworker is only as sharp as his tools, and that's doubly true for woodturners.

Consider a 10-inch bowl blank rotating on the lathe at a modest 600 RPM. The rim of the blank travels at 1570 feet per minute, or about 18 miles per hour. Modern tool steel is amazingly tough and durable, but that's the same as powering the sharp edge of a gouge through almost quarter-mile of wood, every minute. No steel could stay sharp for very long.

That's why the lathe demands sharp tools, and why every would-be woodturner needs to develop a workable sharpening system. Fortunately, as this volume will show, there are several good technologies and approaches. For beginners it is a matter of choosing your sharpening procedure, making the investment to acquire the technology, and learning how to use it. Which is where this little book comes in.

It's a common beginner mistake to turn for too long before sharpening, and consequently to become exasperated by poor results. The cure is simple: learn how to sharpen, and sharpen often. Sharpen before you think the tool is dull, not after.

---

## Selected Readings from *AW Journal*

From its founding in 1986, the American Association of Woodturners has published a regular journal of advice, information, and good fellowship for everyone interested in the field. Led by a series of dedicated editors and board members, the *AW Journal* has evolved to become *American Woodturner* magazine, now published in full color six times each year.

The *AW Journal* is a genuine treasure-trove of practical, shop-tested information written by woodturners for their fellow woodturners. *Sharpening Turning Tools* is part of an ongoing series being extracted from this archive. *Sharpening Turning Tools* is available as a 72-page printed book, or as a download that is readable on all your electronic devices.

Safe woodturning is fun woodturning. A little time spent with this book will help you build strong skills at the lathe while teaching you best woodturning practices.

# Learn to Sharpen All Your Turning Tools

*Alan Lacer*

Were these your first experiences in sharpening turning tools?

- You believed the tools came ready to use?
- You thought because the ad said you could turn 4,822 bowls without sharpening, they weren't kidding?
- When you did try grinding, the surfaces looked like a flint-chipped arrowhead?
- In frustration, you went out and spent several hundred dollars for every grinding jig on the market, only to discover they had not reached the level of a pencil sharpener?
- You sent your tools to a sharpening service only to have them sharpened like a saw blade?

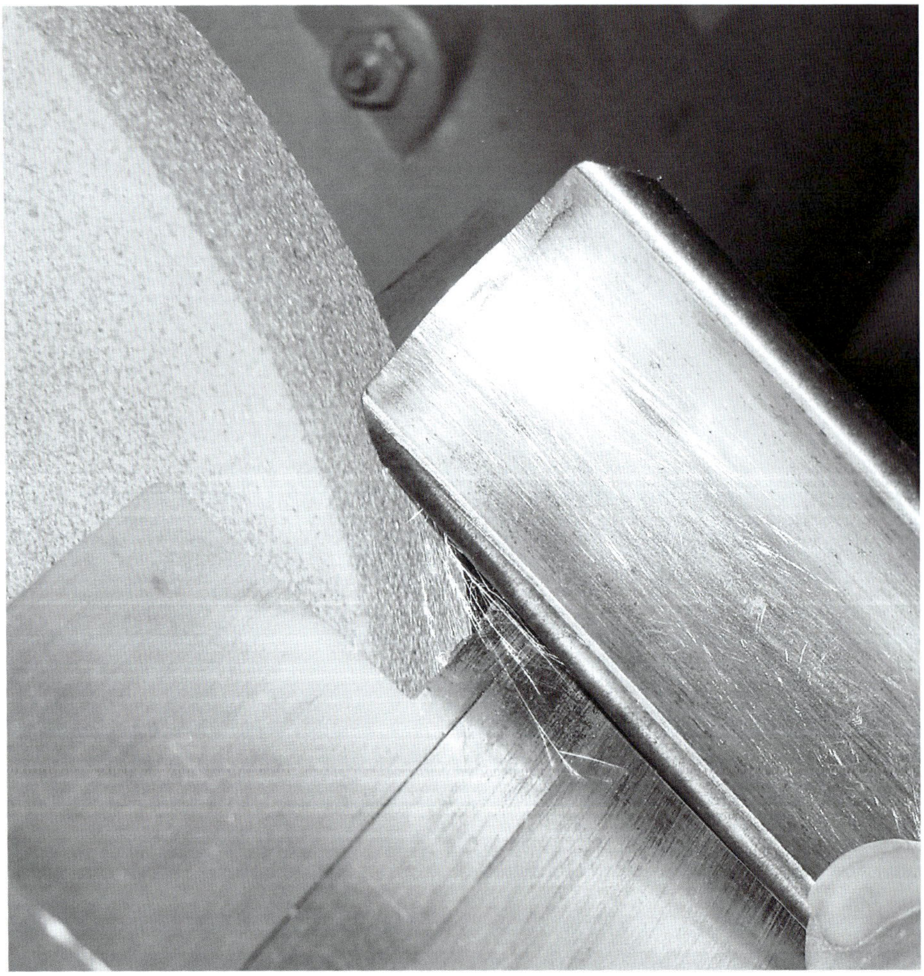

Don't be too bashful in grinding tools. You really can't hurt them—you only shorten them.

Sharpening takes some knocks because some turners see it as a task or chore to be endured and not as a skill—just like turning—that will take time to learn. The good news is that sharpening is closely related to the skill of woodturning.

At one time every conceivable woodworker learned sharpening skills as part of their activity—whether it be sharpening saw blades, axes, spokeshaves, chisels, or plane irons. Today however, few cabinet or furnituremakers sharpen circular or bandsaw blades, planer and joiner knives, router bits or shaper cutters—either these are throwaways or cutting tools sent to specialty shops. Even the other domain where sharpening was essential to learn—that of carving—has often been replaced by spinning bits and cutters that require no sharpening, just replacement. Alas, the poor woodturner still must learn to sharpen. However, there are numerous benefits from learning this skill.

AW 18:3, p52, AW 18:4, p56

Here's how sharpening skills mimic woodturning: You take a turning tool and place it on a tool rest, it meets a round object approaching the edge, and you manipulate the cutting edge. Sounds like what we do as turners, right? Learn the skill to sharpen and you are learning turning—and vice versa.

If sharpening frustrates you, you may need to adopt a tried and true learning strategy: a progression from simple and relatively easy activities to something difficult and more complex. If you think about it, this is how most skills are acquired. If you take up playing the fiddle, you don't start with the Brahms violin concerto as your first task. You probably start with playing notes, then scales, *Yankee Doodle*, and finally progress in difficulty at the rate of your learning. The same path that works for learning math, cooking, computers, golf, drawing, driving, and sailing holds true of sharpening turning tools.

The good news to all of this is that learning those simple tasks first has several benefits: Most of those tasks are also foundational—not just easy—and will be the basis for learning the more difficult maneuvers.

I wonder how many folks have quit woodturning over the years because they either could not sharpen the tools or found they spent more time sanding than turning? So, if you are early on in your career as a turner or you are still frustrated about this sharpening thing, join me and try this progressive order of learning to sharpening your tools.

To begin with, you can't shape and sharpen your tools by hand. We can certainly hone the tools by hand—but honing only keeps a sharp tool sharp or regains a small loss of keenness on a cutting-type turning tool.

*Working with dull tools is like trying to drive your car with flat tires—it just isn't very satisfying.*

No, power equipment is the order of the day for a host of reasons, not the least of which is the type of tool steels used today. Most turning tools currently being sold are not just higher heat-working steels but also higher wear-resistant steels. Your grandpappy's Arkansas oil stone is going to have a tough go on a Glaser V-15 tool or on most of the English, Canadian, and Australian tools now on the market. And the fact that too many tools need major reshaping from their new condition, we will need some power assistance to do the job.

## Buying your grinder and wheels

I find that it is not as simple as "anything will work" for a grinder. If you have a 3600 rpm grinder with a 120-grit gray wheel, 1/2" wide and worn down to 4" in diameter—it will be tough sledding. Nor do I find the slow speed water grinders to be my first choice for a grinder. Ditto for a belt or disc sander either. At least 90 percent of the turners I know worldwide use a wheel grinder—and for good reason.

Here's my grinder preference: an 8" dry wheel grinder, with either variable speed or a fixed rate of 1725 (or 1800), a rock-solid tool rest system, and at least one decent wheel. The 8" wheel offers a lot over smaller and larger wheels: the 8" has 25 percent more surface area than a 6" wheel per revolution. This translates to greater efficiency, cooler grinding, and a much longer wear period before replacement. The 10" and greater diameter wheels leave too little of a hollow-grind for me—and I use the concave surface as a two-point honing jig (see Spring 2002 article).

I prefer the dry wheel as the action is towards me—this allows me to determine a lot of things from the spark trail: where I am grinding, the degree of grinding, and when to stop grinding (sparks just trail over the top of the tool). With a water-type grinder, the action is away from

Strong and sturdy tools rests, good lighting, solid mounting and at least one good wheel are minimal requirements for a reliable grinder. The tool rest on the left is an after-market rest. A supporting strap was added to the right rest for increased rigidity.

me and there is no longer a spark trail. Those grinders are fantastic for carbon-steel tools like plane irons, cabinet makers chisels, scissors and the like—but not a first choice with most turners. I like the slower 1725 speed for a grinder. As I aim to remove minimal material, the 1725 speed grinder has a cooler action, and I just find it a more gentle action than a 3600 rpm screamer (those seem to double my mistakes!). We are now seeing two-speed grinders and infinitely adjustable grinders on the market, which will probably be common with most grinders at some point.

If the tool rest assembly is flimsy, I cannot consistently grind my tools nor is it really safe to do so. Place your thumb in the center of the tool rest of your grinder and push down. You should feel virtually zero give—if it feels springy, improve or replace. You can add extra support strapping, build a wooden rest, or purchase one of several after-market accessory rests. Also, the rest should be adjustable both in angle and the ability to slide towards the stone to accommodate for wear as well as keeping the rest close to the stone for safety purposes. Finally, a light is a worthwhile accessory to the grinder if one did not come attached to it.

## Thoughts on grinding wheels and dressers

First, work with the widest wheel you can fit to your grinder. In most cases this is 3/4" or 1"—but the wider the better. Next, throw away your gray wheels. Spend a lot or spend a little, but acquire at least one decent grinding wheel to sharpen with.

The wheels I would suggest are friable aluminum oxide—now in patriotic colors of red (okay, often pink), white, and blue. The word "friable" refers to the ability of the stone to fracture, exposing fresh grinding surfaces as you use it. Gray wheels usually are not very friable, the cutting particles round over, thus reducing grinding ability and often glazing and generating considerable heat. The color code of these wheels makes them easy to spot. However, there really is a difference between a $10 wheel and $100 wheel.

My advice: If you have an 8" grinder look for wheels that sell for between $25 and $55 and you'll be fine. Two other critical aspects of the wheels: grit size and hardness. I like to work with two different grits on my grinder. For initial shaping of a tool or any other heavy grinding operation, I rely on a 36- or 46-grit wheel. For the actual process of sharpening an edge, I prefer either a 60- (the new 54-grits are close enough) or 80-grit. My ideal setup is a 60-grit on the left side of my grinder (I am right handed; reverse this if you are a lefty) and a 36-grit on the other side.

And finally, how hard should the stone be? Most stones—but not some of the real cheapies—indicate the hardness as shown in the photo. This makes a difference in its friable quality and how well it performs on tougher steels. Stone hardness follows the alphabet scale from soft to hard as you go down the alphabet. Most of the stones commonly found range from H through K. My first choice is a J followed by the K.

Almost as critical as a good stone is a dresser. These are tools that perform a number of functions: true the wheel to the axis of your grinder, flatten the face of the wheel, remove the buildup of metal particles, and expose or sharpen the abrasive particles. There are several choices: star-wheel, gray dressing stick, boron carbide stick, and diamond. I prefer the multiple diamond dresser (not a single point) in a round or tee shape. Keep it by the grinder, and use it lightly but frequently.

Finally, deal with the hazards associated with tool grinding. One of the greatest hazards is to protect yourself from flying particles, whether they are grit from the wheel or pieces of steel removed in

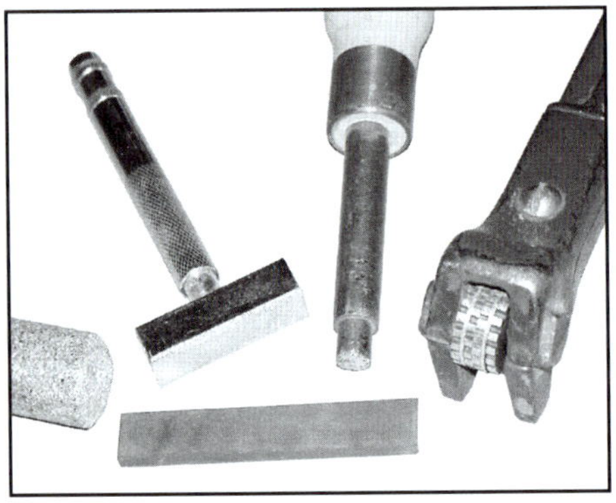

Wheel dresser examples left to right: gray dressing stick, tee diamond, round diamond, star-wheel. In the foreground is a boron carbide stick.

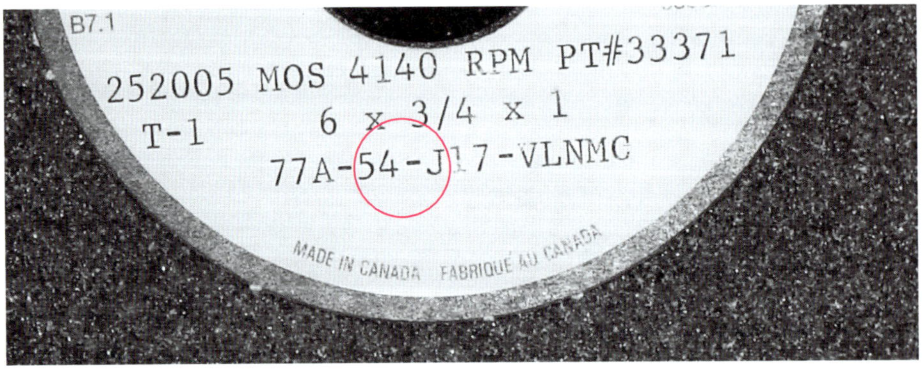


It is challenging to look at a wheel and guess its grit size and hardness. Most stones have a code—in this case, the bottom row of numbers.The most important codes to a turner are circled. The "54" designates grit size; "J" indicates the hardness designation.

the grinding process. The plastic shields on most grinders are worthless to see through after a short time—a full face shield is my first choice followed by goggles. Only use a grinder with metal shrouds to contain the wheel just in case it shatters into pieces.

Another serious hazard is the dust produced from grinding. I like to think of it as ground up glass. I know of no turners who use a wet dust collecting system to direct the grinding dust into—but this is more common with jewelers and other metal workers. And, of course, don't direct the dust into your normal wood dust collecting system—think of the drama of sparks and wood dust meeting!

What is most common is to wear a quality respirator, one rated for small particulate matter. And finally, keep the pinch and crush factor to a minimum by always working with the tool rest as close to the wheel as possible.

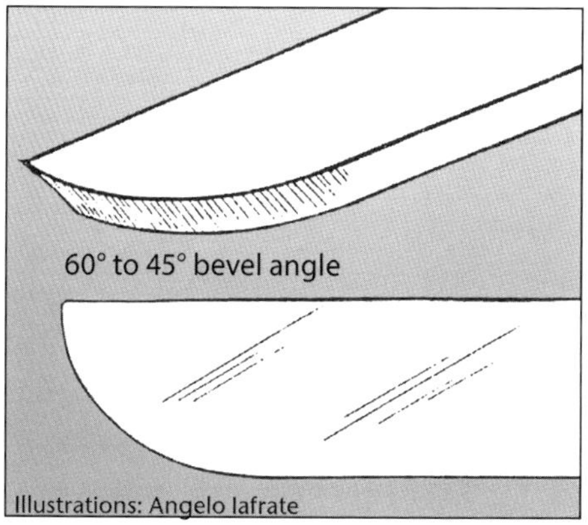

One version of a side-cutting scraper

## Order of learning

From my own learning and watching hundreds of students try to learn the sharpening process, I recommend learning the turning tools in this order:

1. **Scrapers** (all shapes, but not including profile scrapers)
2. **Parting Tools**
3. **Skew Chisels** We'll cover the above tools in this issue.
4. **Roughing Gouges**
5. **Detail Gouges**
6. **Bowl Gouges**

## 1. Sharpening scrapers

These are tools, of almost any shape, that are intended primarily to cut with a burr and not rub the bevel on the wood. Yes, I know we violate both of those guidelines from time to time, but that does not help someone who is starting out. Of all the turning tools, scrapers are some of the most straightforward to sharpen. Few turners struggle with these tools in getting the basic process, and we don't have to be too fussy about shapes, angles, and multi facets on the ground face.

The first rule of sharpening turning tools: Profile the tool first, then pull a bevel up to meet that profile. For a scraper, personal preference determines the shape. You will probably discover that the slight dome on a new "round nose" scraper you just bought isn't very rounded. You may even find you don't use one side of the rounded end, so it may take on the shape of

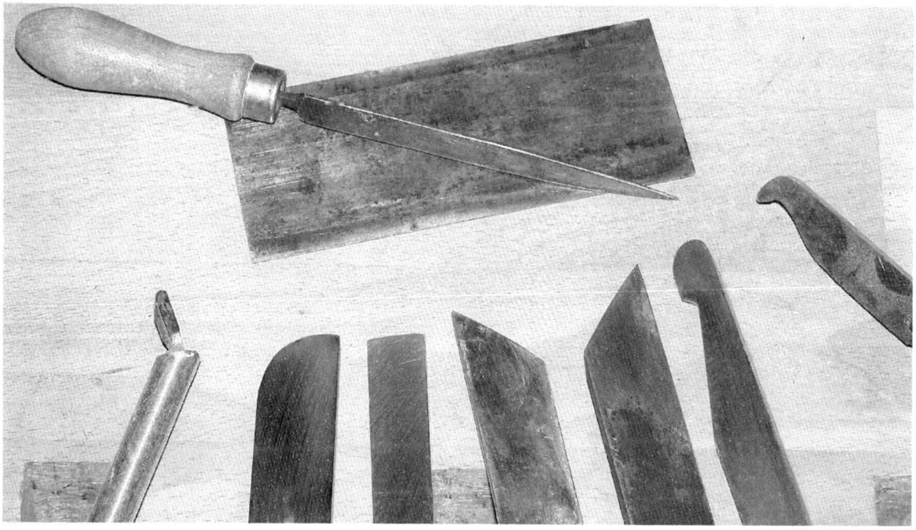
Woodturning scraping tools are quite similar to the cabinetmaker's scrapers (background, shown with a burnisher). Both types of scrapers usually cut with a burr and both can make use of a burnisher to raise that burr. Turning scrapers are thicker and heavier in weight and come (or can be made into) in an array of shapes for specific purposes.

a side-ground scraper. Whatever the specific need or your style of turning, shape the tool first.

Next, rough in the bevel angle. When most of these tools are new, I find the bevel to be 80 to even 90 degrees below the cutting edge. I believe manufacturers started with the notion that a scraper needs a lot of support under the edge since you don't have the secondary fulcrum of a bevel-rubbing tool to add extra support (your tool rest is the primary fulcrum). Unless your scrapers are 1/8" thick, this is a bad notion.

As a matter of fact, if I am using the tool at a scraping angle (with no bevel support) and the bevel inadvertently touches the wood, I can get a catch. I treat the bevels on scrapers as clearance angles, so mine are ground between 45 to 60 degrees. I also don't have to worry about single facets and a hollow grind on the ground bevel: I don't hone the bevel on these tools so it is not as critical as it is with other turning tools. However, grinding uniform bevels on these tools is great practice for all the tools to follow.

The process for sharpening is straightforward. After profiling, proceed to grind the bevel to match the profile. If you need some assistance early on in sharpening, set the tool rest angle to that 45- to 60-degree window. Start at the back of the bevel, keeping the tool flat on the rest, and progress along the cutting edge until sparks just come over the top. I don't look for a heavy stream of sparks, but consistent "tracer bullets" that tell me I have reached the cutting surface.

Being a scraper, the raised burr will be my cutting edge at least 90 percent of the time. I can use the burr right off of the grinder (useful if heavy stock removal is called for) or remove that burr with a flat stone and pull up a new burr with a cabinetmaker's burnisher or the honing stone.

By using one of the other methods, I find it easier to produce different types of burrs—some for heavy work, some for fine finishing work. In those cases where the burr is too aggressive for a particular piece of wood (you may feel it "picking" at the wood rather than a smooth leveling action), try scraping with a sharp edge—produced by grinding—then removing the burr on top with a flat honing stone. This is similar to the action of scraping with the edge of a knife or the furnituremaker scraping the top of a table with a large piece of broken glass. When you work a sharp edge in a scraping action, it may quickly dull the edge. However for that window of doing fine scraping, it may be just the ticket.

## 2. Parting tools

There are several variations of this tool, but the most common is a rectangular section of steel with the cutting edge in the middle that's ground on both sides. This is a great tool to learn cutting tool sharpening as it has a relatively small area to grind (the edge is usually no greater than 1/4") and the edge is in a flat plane.

For profiling, make sure the edge is ground straight across, and the included angles of the ground bevels are around 25 degrees. Fortunately, new parting tools most often arrive profiled in an acceptable manner—not sharp mind you, but routinely shaped fine. To sharpen, either set the tool rest at the approximate angle desired, use the edge of the rest as a steady, or use your fingers to adjust the angle.

Start at the back of the bevel (called the "heel"), keep the edge horizontal, and lap from side to side on the wheel until you just see sparks trailing over the top of

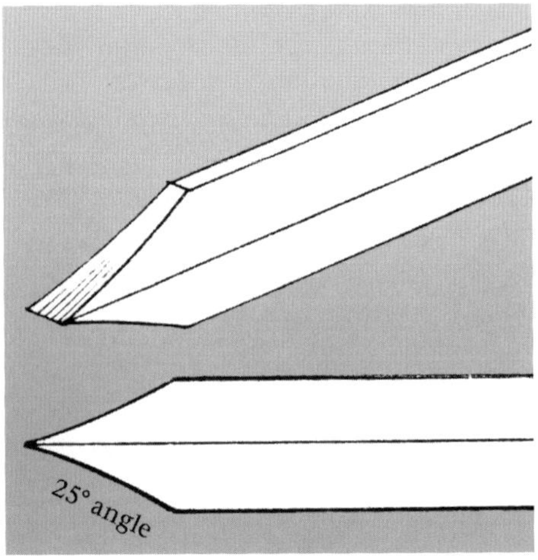


Diamond-section parting tool (profile and angles same as rectangular tool)

the cutting edge. Flip over the tool and repeat the same procedure on the other side. The objective is to produce a single facet with a slight hollow grind. If your movements are controlled and steady, this all happens. If jerky, uneven, inconsistent, too much pressure, "grind and look" and "grind and look," then things probably won't be so good.

Go slow, be deliberate, leave the tool on the wheel, and use only enough pressure as it takes to keep the tool from bouncing on the rest. I am always surprised how much of grinding and turning is really about feeling your way along rather than seeing.

In grinding, most of the action is on the other side of what you can see. We can help the looking part along—especially when learning the process—by placing our head to the side of the grinder or by the use of a mirror (attributed to a North Carolina turner). In time, most of your grinding will be by feel and watching the spark trail to give the additional feedback.

## 3. Skew chisels

Fortunately, the sharpening of a skew chisel is similar to the parting tool: two ground flat planes that meet to form a cutting edge. The only real difference is in the skewed angle of the cutting end—essentially a clearing and viewing advantage over a square-across chisel.

Again, profile the tool first. For a "traditional" straight-edged skew, I recommend 70 degrees from point to point. Rather than measuring included angles to measure the steepness of the two ground bevels, I use the thickness of the steel as the reference. Using this method, grind the bevels back to approximately 1.5 times the thickness of the blade.

For the sharpening process, follow these steps: Keep the edge horizontal and parallel to the face of the wheel, start at the heel and lap back and forth. Continue this process until sparks just trail over the edge. Flip over the tool and repeat the same procedure.

If you have an "oval style" skew (my last choice for a skew) you will find it wants to wobble rather than remain in a flat plane. In that case, maintain pressure in the center of the tool with a thumb to essentially lock it into a fixed plane. As an alternative, investigate a grinding jig that locks the darn thing in place.

If you are grinding a curved-edged skew, simply grind the edge while it is generally parallel to the face of the wheel. This will require a rotational motion that follows the curve of the edge. If the skew plagues you with multiple facets, go ahead and set the tool rest to the suggested bevel angle. Keep the tool flat on the rest and follow the above strategies. I have had good success just using the front or back edge of the tool rest as a point to slide along for a straight skew or to pivot on while grinding a curved edge.

Until you have a sense of where you are grinding on the tool, it's helpful to either place your head to the side of the wheel or make use of a small mirror. The mirror, shown above, allows you to see your placement of the tool on the wheel.

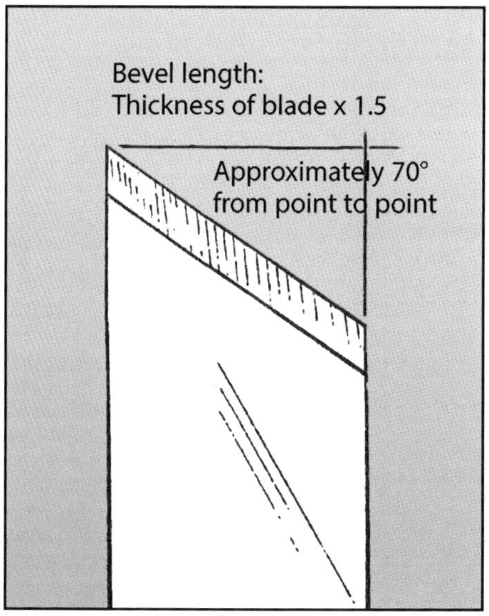


Typical grinding of a skew chisel

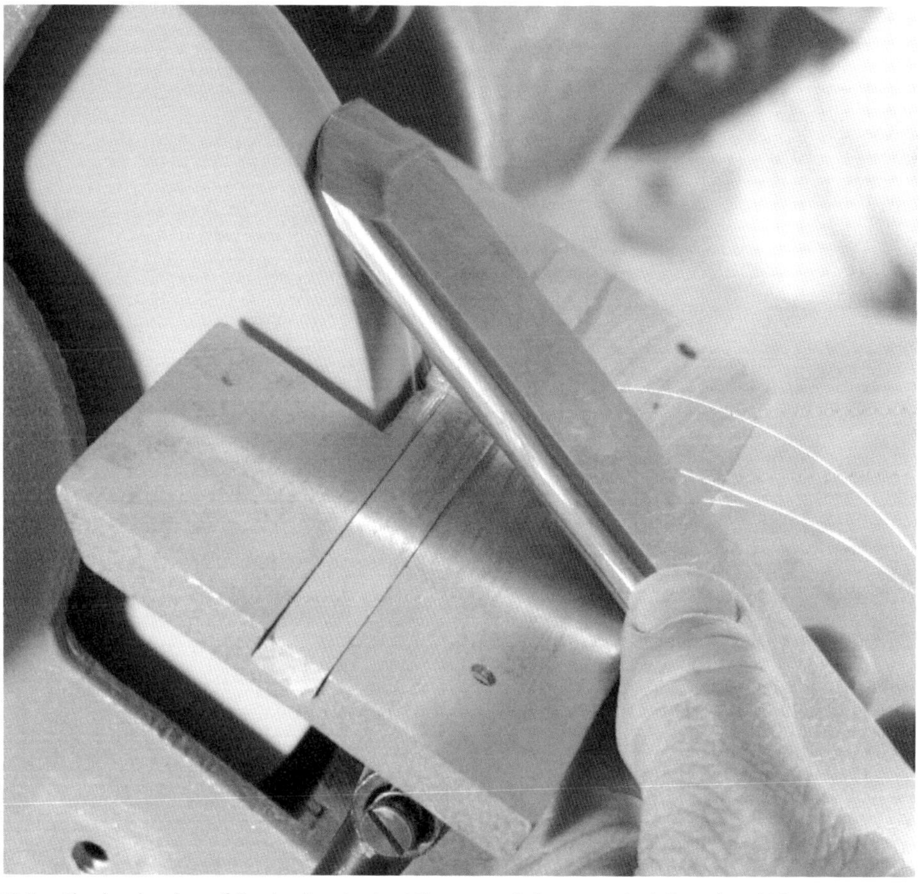

Using the back edge of the tool rest, pivot the curved skew to grind the edge. Using a rotational movement, grind in the area that is roughly parallel to the face of the wheel.

## Tests for sharpness of cutting tools

If you can see the edge, there is no edge. Short of turning, this is the best test I know. Use an incandescent light to check for any reflection along the edge; a sharp edge disappears into a black line. Dull spots will reflect light.

What comes off the tool, dust or curls? Even in dry material, a sharp tool forms a longer chip or ribbon, dull tools produce dust or very short chips.

How much effort does it require to remove the material? Unless you are roughing out a large piece, a sharp tool presented at the right angle is almost effortless; a dull tool requires more force.

What does the cutting action sound like? A sharp tool makes a sound reminiscent of a sharp hand plane; the dull tool sounds flat or makes a scraping sound.

*If you can see the edge, there is no edge.*

How clean is the surface when you stop the lathe for inspection? Sometimes it is a difficult piece of wood, but generally a sharp tool gives far superior results to the surface of the wood.

## 4. Spindle roughing gouge

The spindle roughing gouge is perhaps the friendliest gouge to use and one of the easiest to sharpen. It differs from all the previous tools (Fall 2003 issue) as we are now into curved edges. Traditionally, the tool is a deep U-shape with a straight across cutting edge.

Profiling is fairly straight forward. Make sure the tool is straight across when viewed from the top and viewed from the side. You can have the top corners canted back a few degrees, but not canted forward (a forward cant will make a more aggressive tool). The bevel angle should be approximately 45 degrees.

Sharpening begins at one corner, with the heel of the bevel touching the wheel and the cutting edge parallel to the face of the wheel. Rotate the tool in the same curved plane until you reach the other corner, then return to the point where you began by rotating backwards (but still grinding) to your original motion. I tend to repeat these motions until I have lapped all the way to the cutting edge. Stop when the sparks just trail over the top of the edge.

## Notes on overheating the tool

By now you may have come up against the problem of bluing the grinding surface of the tool. If you have high-carbon steel tools, you have a problem: the steel has now been re-tempered to a hardness that is too soft to hold an edge for woodturning. If you have high-speed or high-heat-working tool steel—no problem. But how do you know what kind of steel?

Generally the high-carbon tool steels produce a complex, white, bursting spark when placed on the grinding wheel. The high-speed steels tend to have individual, orange sparks. Often the manufacturer stamps the handle or steel itself with "HSS" or "High Speed Steel." I have found some inexpensive imported tools stamped with those designations, but sparked like high carbon tools—so be careful.

Here are some suggestions regarding overheating. First, learn to grind with a lightness of hand and movement of tool that does not overwork an area, thereby reducing heat. Second, use friable wheels that grind cooler, and dress the wheel often. If you have carbon steel tools—and some of my old favorites are of that steel—quench in water frequently for heavy grinding or delicate points of skew chisels.

If you have high-speed tools, don't quench in water: the effect may be too shocking for the steel and possibly produce small fractures at the cutting edge. The high-speed steels easily handle temperatures of 700 to 1000 degrees F with no loss of hardness (bluing is around 580 degrees F). If the high-speed tools get too hot to handle (during heavy grinding), I just place them on a large metal heat sink like a lathe bed and take a short break. The best rule for all steels is learn to work without generating a lot of excessive heat and eliminate the need for quenching.

## *Grind the bevel and not the edge.*

On the larger roughing gouges, some turners like to work about one third of the edge at a time until that section is fully sharpened. They make one final pass along the entire length of the bevel to blend it all together. The biggest problem turners seem to have is moving the tool edge in and out when trying to rotate the tool through that large curved plane. Use your fingers to create an artificial plane to lock the tool in. If you have trouble staying in that 45 degree bevel zone, set the angle of the tool rest and maintain downward pressure to keep the tool flat and thereby in the correct orientation.

If by chance you have a large shallow gouge (3/4" or larger) that was packaged in your tool set as a roughing gouge, here are my suggestions. Odds are pretty good it has a domed edge (maybe almost looks like your thumbnail). You might consider simply grinding it straight across and sharpening as suggested for the deep-fluted roughing gouge.

If you decide to leave it with that "fingernail" look—in order to do some detailing work such as large coves or beads— then approach it the way you would the detail gouge.

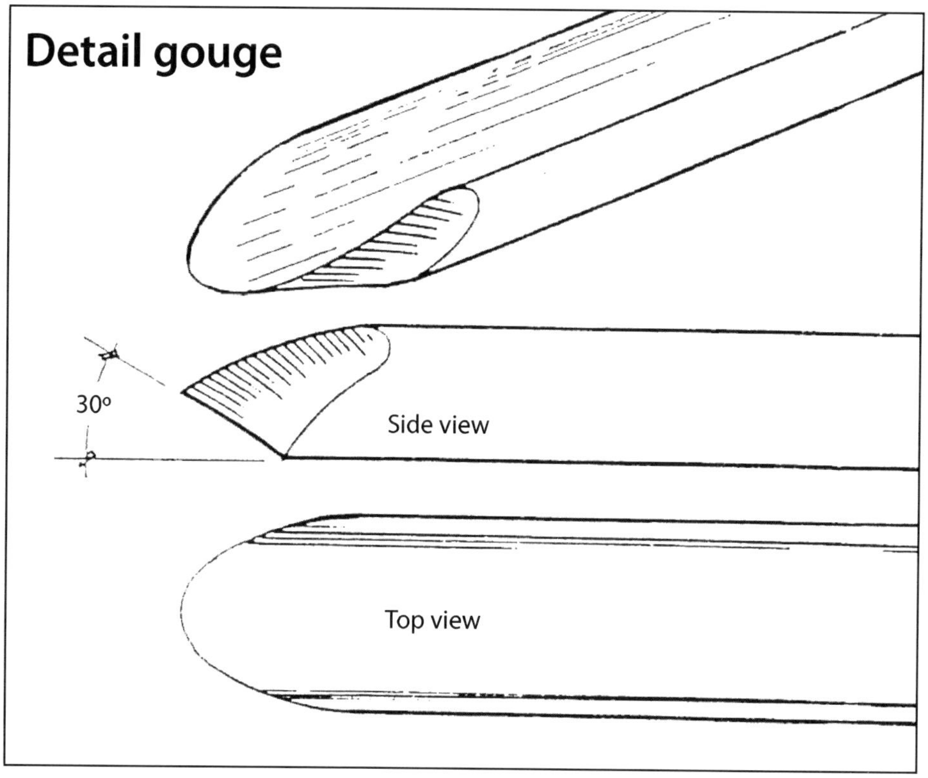


## 5. Detail gouge

What's in a name? A shallow fluted gouge with a fingernail shape--primarily designed for spindle work and used for detailing work--will be the same tool no matter what we call it. I wish we could some day standardize a few names for turning tools, but that's a lot to ask for. This tool goes by at least four names: detail gouge, spindle gouge, shallow gouge, and fingernail gouge. All of these names point to some truth about it, but still leads to much confusion. For this article, it's a detail gouge.

This detail gouge is probably the first tool to get your goat. (It

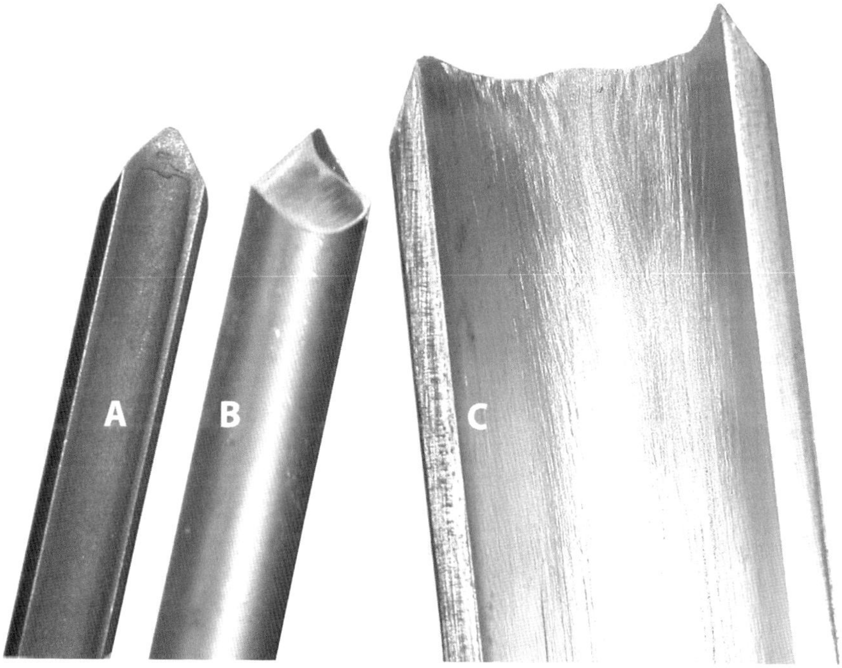


At right are improperly ground gouges:

**A**: A detail gouge ground too pointy. This is caused by either rotating the entire tool parallel to the face of the grinding wheel (as with a roughing gouge), or over grinding the sides.

**B**: A bowl gouge ground on the side with a concave profile. This makes an aggressive tool and one that does a poor job of leveling if used to shear scrape.

**C**: A roughing gouge overground along the edge. This most often shows up as a jagged or saw-toothed edge.

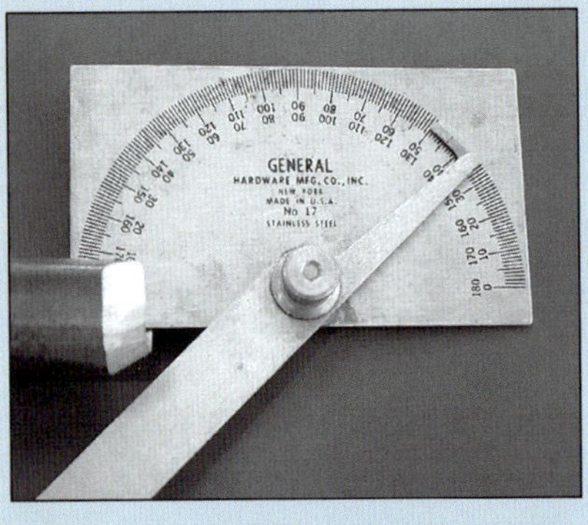


**Give a protractor a try.**

We got a few letters after last issue's grinding article about grinding the correct angle. This metal protractor—available for about $12—is one inexpensive and reliable solution.

was the first tool I'm aware of that a grinding jig was developed to do the sharpening.) No tricks of setting the tool rest at the right angle will help, nor will simply rotating the tool back and forth. Nope, we now have a tool that is in an oval plane with the steel below the edge in varying thicknesses.

Let me explain. If I shape the tool into a fingernail shape, orient the tool with the flute facing the grinding wheel, and rotate it along a circular path that is parallel to the face of the wheel, I will probably produce a pointy or "spear-pointed" cutting edge that is not very versatile nor friendly to the user.

Profiling is essential to the detail tool. It performs astutely in forming concave and convex forms in between center work or details on feet, bases and rims of bowl and vessel work. The shallow draft of its flute (a low "sweep" if we are talking to carvers) allows the tool to sneak in between details, often on its side and do its fine work.

The deep fluted roughing gouges and bowl gouges have trouble detailing elements that are close together. So, the detail profile should reflect its intended activities. Establish a fingernail shape to the cutting edge—thus making the detail gouge more of a side-cutting tool, especially when rotated on its side.

Just as your fingernail would not grow to a point, so must the end of the tool not be too pointy. The analogy with the fingernail is a good one: the smaller the gouge the more it is like a little fingernail; the larger the gouge the more it is domed like a thumbnail. I like to profile by holding the tool nearly flat on a tool rest set to about 90 degrees to the wheel. Gauge your progress by the view from above—striving to get a balanced radius on both sides of the tool (see illustration). Next, rough in an approximate bevel angle of 30 degrees. This flatter angle reflects the need of the tool to fit between details while in use.

There are several strategies for matching the edge to the profile, but I will give you the easiest one for me. Treat the bevel of the tool as having three parts: a middle section, and a right and left side. Start by holding the tool with the flute pointed up, contacting the bevel heel in the middle section. This will be the basis for all detail grinding, and the reference point for grinding of the bevel middle area or sides.

With a push up and rotation to the right, move the tool to the left side of the wheel. Grind as you reverse this action and return to the original starting point. When both sides show sharpness from the spark trail, blend the center section into each side.

## 6. Bowl gouges

I recommend tackling bowl gouges last, but not because they're extraordinarily difficult. In major reshaping, you'll remove considerable amounts of steel. Plus, bowl gouges have at least one tricky grind that causes some problems.

*A sharp tool at the right cutting angle is virtually effortless.*

The preferred profile is one of personal choice. Most turners use one of three common grinds. What I term "traditional" is shaped exactly like a roughing gouge—and the sharpening is attended to in the same manner, only easier because of the reduced size. The "transitional" is one favored by many bowl turners, and may be the only profile you require on a bowl gouge. Careful study of the diagram shows it to be close to the fingernail shape we put on the detailing gouge. The side profile should be straight or a bit convex—just avoid concave. Once profiled, I sharpen in the same manner as the detail gouge.

The bowl grind that has launched more than a few commercial and shop-made jigs is the Irish grind. Although it looks formidable with such a long edge, it is in truth quite tame—if you have a strategy. Get the profile correct from above, the side, and rough in the steep bevel angle on the nose. Then divide the tool into three sections: the two long sides and the front nose. Grind the sides nearly parallel to the face of the stone. Finally, grind the small front section with the same technique for the detail gouge. I finish with a little blending of the nose into the sides.

## Tests for sharpness of cutting tools

- If you can see the edge there is no edge. Short of actually turning, this is the best test I know. Use an incandescent light to check for any reflection along the edge. A sharp edge disappears into a black line; dull spots reflect light.
- What comes off the tool—dust or curls? Even in dry material, a sharp tool forms a longer chip or ribbon while dull tools produce dust or short chips.
- How much effort does it require to remove the material? Unless you are roughing out a large piece, a sharp tool presented at the right angle is almost effortless; a dull tool requires more force.
- How does the cutting action sound? A sharp tool makes a sound reminiscent of a sharp hand plane; the dull tool sounds flat or makes a scraping sound.
- How clean is the surface when you stop the lathe for inspection? Generally a sharp tool gives far superior results to the surface of the wood.

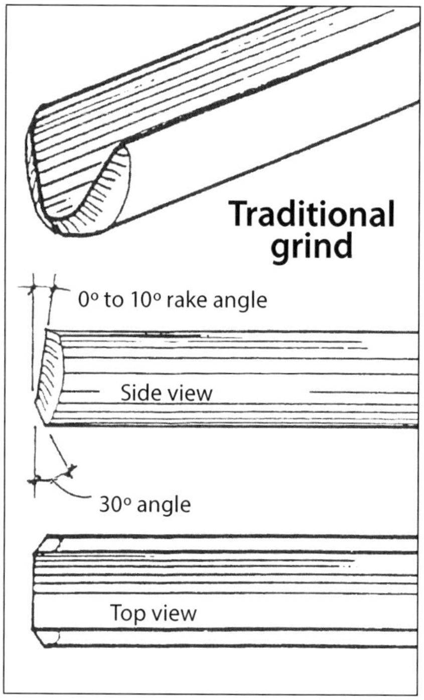


A traditional (fingernail) grind has some sound applications: the outside of a face grain bowl when mounted backwards (base is at tailstock side) or for opening the interior of a bowl (opening is now facing tailstock side).

## Two ways to sharpen a bowl gouge

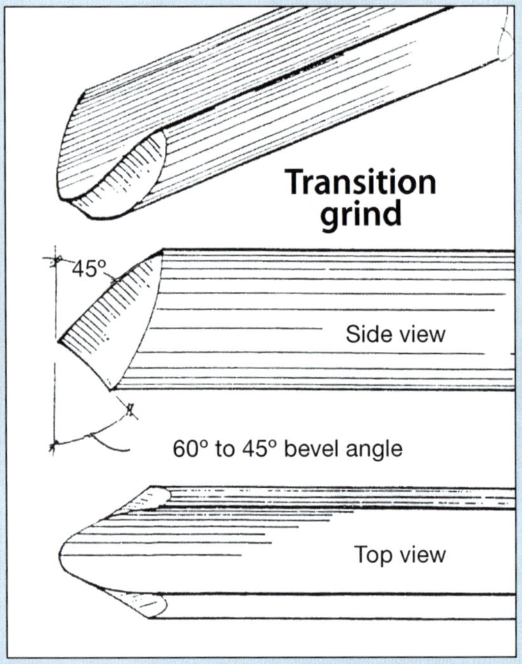


I recommend the transition grind for new bowl turners. You work the outside of a face grain bowl regardless of the orientation. The ground sides provide the opportunity to do a little shear scraping.

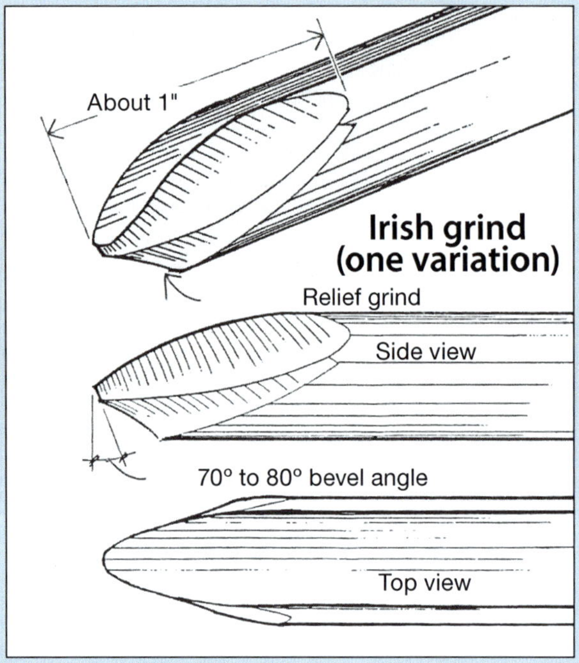


Experienced turners may prefer the more-complicated Irish grind. It's a good roughing tool for bowls, a detailing tool with the elliptical front, a shear-scraping tool, and a tool to make a smoother transition from sides to bottom.

### Grinding jigs

This is perhaps sacrilegious, but I am not a big fan of the grinding jigs. I still find most individuals learn sharpening with no other "jig" than their tool rest and hands—at least for most tools.

But is there a place for the grinding jigs? Yes! For those folks who cannot seem to learn freehand grinding, those with physical limitations, those who need a crutch to get started (like training wheels on your first bike), those sharpening a large number of tools for others (some classroom or manufacturing situations), or those one or two difficult tools you just can't seem to get at all or consistently. If you fall into one of these camps, get a jig—but at least learn to resharpen your tools by hand when all that is needed is a light refreshing. The information in this article applies to most aspects of sharpening whether you do it freehand or with a grinding jig. Be forewarned though, jigs still require considerable judgment.

*Alan Lacer (www.woodturninglearn.net) is a turner, writer, and instructor living near River Falls, WI.*

A jig may be helpful in some situations of learning to grind.

# Shaping Tool Edges

*David Ellsworth*

Over time, most turners develop a working familiarity with their tools, or at least a certain confidence in knowing what a tool is supposed to do and how to make it work. But when it comes to understanding why a tool works (or doesn't work), many people begin to scratch their heads. It's that 'why' part that I'd like to address here.

Before I get to tool applications, let me begin with some basic concepts of tool design that affect all tools. For instance: You get up in the morning and shave. Before lunch, you grab your ax and go cut down a tree to turn. Then, after a nice nap, you buck up the sections with a splitting maul. The razor, the ax, and the maul are all cutters in some form. They each have a specific function and are very effective tools, but neither can be used to perform the function of the other ... at least not efficiently.

Now, look at the edges of these tools in cross section and think of the similarities between the razor and a skew, the ax and a gouge, the mall and a scraper. They all have two surfaces or planes that join to form an edge, and each has a certain amount of mass which supports (or doesn't support) that edge: the maul having the most amount of mass, the razor the least. Obviously, the razor and the skew have a sharper edge, but because they lack mass, these edges just don't stay sharp for very long ... they lack durability.

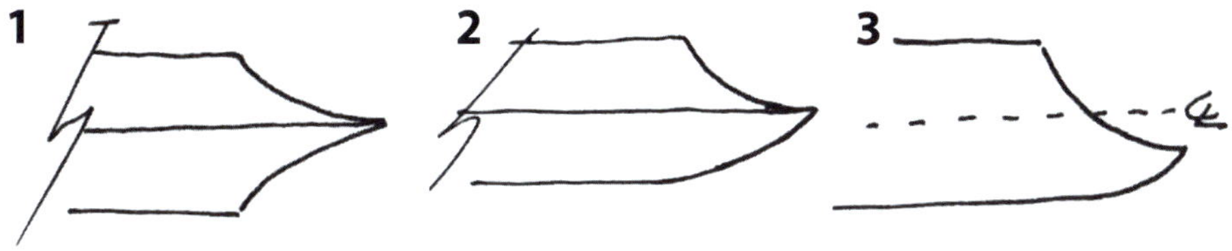


1. Conventional parting tool
2. Modified with convex edge
3. Ellsworth shop-made tool

Specifically, the more mass a tool has to support the edge, the more durable it will be, albeit at the sake of sharpness. Gouges, then, are the compromise between the two. They sacrifice the sharpness of the skew, but they gain durability due to the greater mass supporting the edge.

Friction and abrasion, of course, will cause any tool to lose its sharpness. The various grades of high-speed steel available in today's tools will extend edge-life. But some woods are so abrasive they'll quickly whack the edge off any tool—like root burls, which usually contain pockets of sand, many species of Eucalyptus, which contain silica, or any time you're turning areas of bark that have been impacted with dust from the wind. Spalted woods can be a nightmare, because the black zone lines are not wood anymore. As far as the tool is concerned, they act more like charcoal, and one good slice with your tool and the edge is gone.

Let's look at some practical applications of specific tools to see how this relationship between sharpness and mass applies to cutting efficiency.

## The parting tool

Illustration #1 shows the side view of a conventional diamond shaped parting tool, where the widest part of the tip is in the center of the tool.

Contrast that with Illustration #2, which shows a modification I use for that same tool. The difference is that by grinding a convex shape under the tip, I have introduced a small amount of mass to support the edge. The tip of the modified shape isn't quite as sharp as the original, but it works better because it doesn't vibrate on the wood or burnish as quickly. The result is that it stays sharp longer. Of course, you can't flip it upside down. But, in truth, once the original tool is dull on one side, it doesn't work either way.

Illustration #3 shows the side view of a parting tool I made myself. It's 3/16-in. thick by 5/8-in. wide scraper turned on its edge, and then re-sharpened using the convex/concave idea from the diamond shaped tool. Notice that I've also dropped the tip below the centerline of the tool. This keeps the tool from vibrating when cutting.

AW 16:1, p38

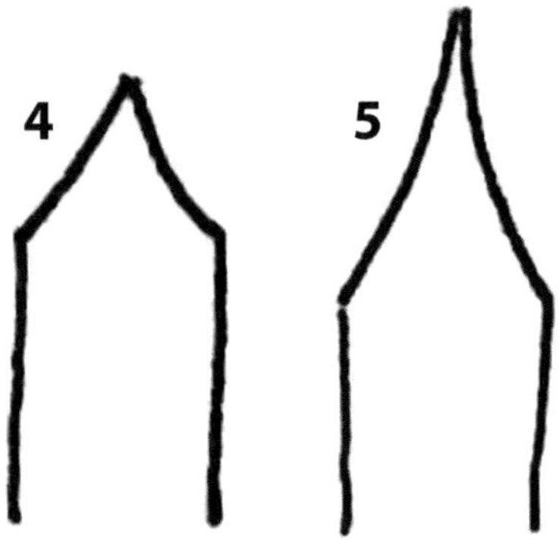


4. Blunt edge factory grind
5. Custom grind: thinner and sharper

## The skew

Illustrations #4 and #5 show the cross section of two skews. The left one, #4, shows how it usually looks straight from the factory with lots of mass behind the tip, but not very sharp. The right one, #5, is the way most turners grind the tip to make it work properly. Once again, while the custom-ground thinner blade shown in #5 is sharper, it lacks durability so it must be re-honed more frequently to keep a fine edge. The difference between the conventional straight-bladed skew, Illustration #6, and the radius, or convex-blade design, Illustration #7, is that the radius skew presents slightly less physical contact of the edge to the wood during the cut. With less of the edge touching

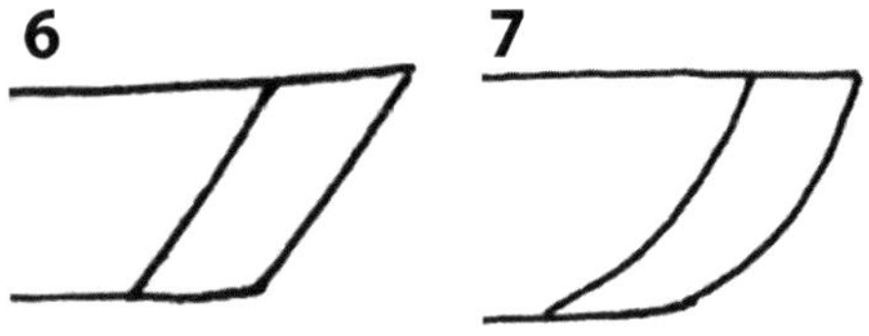


6. Conventional skew
7. Radiused Skew

the wood, and assuming the mass and shape of the two tools is the same, the radius design creates a bit less drag on the wood and, therefore, it gives more energy to the cut.

## The scraper

Illustration #8 shows another side-view example of what many of the

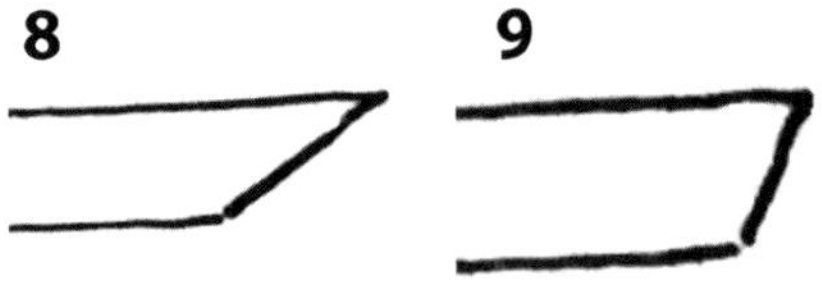


8. Conventional scraper bevel
9. Steeper bevel for finishing cuts

less expensive scrapers look like. Illustration #9 shows the same tool but with a steeper bevel so it can be used to make finishing cuts on the inside of a bowl. The steeper angle of the bevel in Illustration #9 provides more mass for durability, but sacrifices sharpness. To make the tool function, you must add a burr to the edge to do the cutting.

It's worth experimenting with different grit wheels on the grinder to raise this burr. A 60-grit wheel will raise a huge burr that is very aggressive on the wood. But it will also wear away quickly, leaving a jagged edge that clogs up with dust from the wood and stalls the cut. Conversely, a 120-grit wheel may not raise enough of a burr to do the work. In my experience, a coarser burr works well with softer woods and a finer burr works best with harder woods ... but that's only a personal preference, not a rule.

When you are using a small-tipped scraper with deep hollowing tools, you will gain increased control of the tip when the bevel angle is steeper, like the one shown in Illustration #10. The bevel angle shown in Illustration #11 gives a sharper edge to the tip, but is so aggressive that it may be too difficult to control ... it's just one of those odd cases when the tip is too sharp! As well, when using a deep hollowing

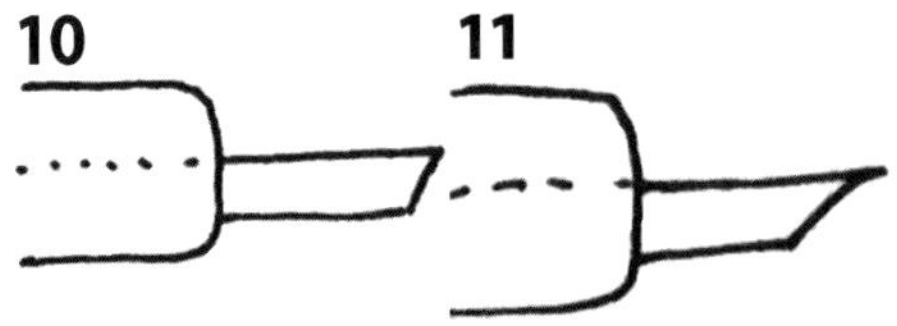


10. Steep bevel gives better control
11. Sharper tip is too aggressive

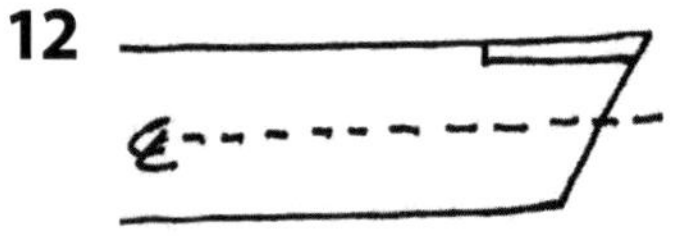


12. Top surface on same plane as top of shaft

scraper with a straight tip, I drop the top surface of the cutter to the centerline of the shaft (Illustration #10) to prevent the tool from grabbing or vibrating on the wood. It's the same principle described above regarding the parting tool. If the top surface of the tip is above the centerline, or on the same plane as the top surface of the shaft (Illustration 12), watch out!

## The gouge

There are many types of gouges including spindle, bowl, deep-fluted, roughing, detail, hook and loop. But the principles of what I'm describing here apply to all. The steep vertical angle of the edge in the gouge shown in Illustration #13 is fine for cutting across the bottom of a deep bowl where you need to keep the bevel in

13. Side view of steep vertical edqe for cutting bottom of bowl

contact with the wood. But it's not as sharp or as versatile as the gouges shown in Illustrations #14a and #14b.

To further illustrate the importance of the relationship of mass to sharpness, we only have to look at what's commonly called the shearing cut, or the shear-scraping cut. This cut can be done either with a gouge with a drawn back edge (Illustration #14b) or a scraper, by placing the edge of the tool approximately 45 degrees diagonally across the surface of the wood. Regardless of which tool is used, it must have a burr on the

14a 14b

14a and 14b. Side view where angles of edges are drawn back to create sharper edges

edge, as a honed edge will simply be burnished away on the first cut. When shear cutting with a tool that has a thin, skew-like cross section, as in Illustration #15, the lack of mass supporting the edge will cause the tool to vibrate on the wood. To eliminate this vibration, simply use a tool with more mass behind the edge, as in Illustration #16.

15 16

15. Thin skew-like edge can cause vibration
16. Additional mass behind edge reduces vibration

Another cause of vibration comes from tools that are thin and very long, like a 1/4-in. gouge that is 8-in. long, or a long skinny parting tool, or a thin-bladed scraper. It seems as if all you have to do is look at these tools and they begin to vibrate, and I wouldn't want to dangle one of them out over the tool rest just to prove my point. With the gouge and the parting tool, I simply cut these tools in half! It may seem like a waste of both steel and money, but at least they work properly. With any of these tools, always keep the tool rest as close as possible to the workpiece to reduce the vibration.

## Should you hone?

To hone or not to hone? Now, that is a good question! Habits and traditions being what they are, honing a tool really depends on what you want the tool to do. I hone all my skews and gouges for spindle turning, because I want a super edge to do the work ... knowing that the edge will quickly burnish away and need to be re-honed. But my preference is not to hone bowl gouges, because a burr edge works fine for rough-cutting both green and dry woods. As well, I use a shearing cut instead of a conventional bevel cut for my final surface and without the burr the shearing cut just won't work.

And I use 100-grit aluminum oxide grinding wheels, because they produce the right size of a burr to do the job and one that doesn't wear away as fast as a burr produced by a 60 or 80 grit wheel.

## Learning to sharpen

As a teacher of woodturning, I would be remiss if I didn't offer a few tips on learning how to sharpen these tools. If you find yourself over-grinding your tools, you're probably learning two basic things: How to raise your level of frustration, and how to waste away a good tool!

Consider that when you go to the grinder, you are NOT trying to sharpen the tool. Instead, you simply want to dress the bevel. If the bevel is properly dressed, the tool will be sharp. It's automatic.

Try this. Turn the grinder off. Bring the tool to the wheel in your usual manner, either with your hands or in a sharpening jig. Make a few slow passes on the non-rotating wheel so that you feel comfortable. Now close your eyes. What you will now feel is your body, and all the tension that has built up in it, mostly in your neck and your hands. Relax that death grip so that your fingers are simply cradling the tool instead of clamped to it. You will also feel your toes, your knees, and all the other body parts that are keeping you from falling over when you grind the tool. Try to re-position your body by spreading your feet apart and unlocking your knees. This will allow you to move freely as you continue to practice the movement of the tool across the wheel. Open your eyes to see if the tool is still in the center of the wheel. Now close them again.

## Release tension

Focus on relieving tension wherever you feel it. What you are learning is the process of grinding, without the tension and without wasting away the tool. Practice this for a minimum of five minutes. It will feel eternal, but you will be forever rewarded.

When you do turn on the grinder, the tension will likely return, so continue to focus on relaxing those areas of the body wherever the tension appears. This takes practice, but the less tension in the body, the lighter your touch will be of the tool to the wheel and the more successful you will be in dressing the bevel. Most important, be conscious not to force the tool against the wheel. You can also practice this method of turning the machine off and closing your eyes on any cut you make on the lathe. It's a wonderful way of learning how to move with the cuts instead of forcing them. And when you're moving properly, everything just seems to work a whole lot better.

*David Ellsworth is a full-time studio woodturner who teaches turning at his home in Pennsylvania. Sketches by the author.*

# Testing the Steel in Turning Tools

*Alan Lacer*

For several thousand years, a piece of steel (or at least a steel-edged tool) came between the woodturner and the wood. Although the skill of the turner is a huge consideration in woodturning, the properties of the turning tool influence such things as longevity of the cutting edge (how long it holds an edge), whether it tends to break or bend easily, and how the tool reacts to heat (whether in use on wood or while grinding).

Since the 1980s, the transition from high-carbon steel woodturning tools (0.5 to just over 2 percent carbon) to high-speed-steel tools (iron, carbon, and additional alloys) is now nearly complete in the sale of new tools.

Few high-carbon steel tools are now available for sale in the USA (usually only from sources of used items and estate sales). High-speed steel (HSS) was developed for the metal trades and has been around for more than 100 years, but is a relatively new steel for the woodturner.

Although steel manufactured in Sheffield, England, dominated the tool market for decades, there has been a flood of HSS turning tools in recent years coming into the market from the Far East (primarily from China).

This influx of inexpensive imported tools, often at a fraction of the price of the English turning tools, really caught my attention. But with spiraling shipping costs and steel prices, how can these tools be sold as high-speed steel (sometimes stated as M2), some at prices below the price of a handle on the English tools?

I wanted to see if at least the steel was the same. The traditional way of determining whether a tool is high-carbon or HSS was with a spark test at the grinder. This test turned out not to be foolproof, as some tools sparked as HSS, but lacked sufficient quantities of those materials that produce the benefits of the genuine article.

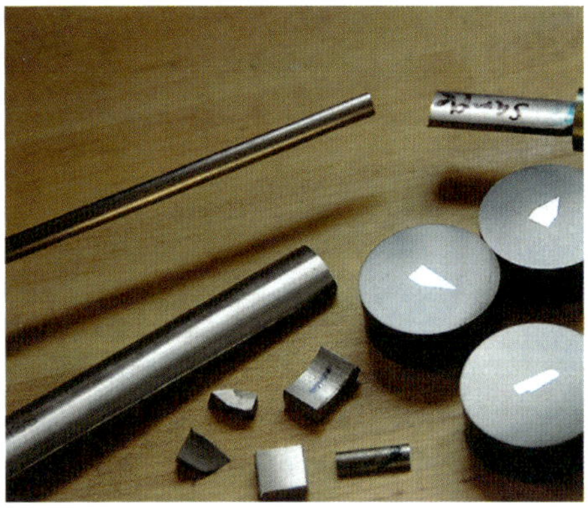

Sections of lathe tools embedded in composite materials and prepared for emission (spark) test.

## Tests at certified lab

The tests were conducted at Stork Material Technology (storksmt.com), a certified laboratory in Huntington Beach, California. The warning at the bottom of each Stork test stated: "The recording of false, fictitious, or fraudulent statements or entries on the certificate may be punishable as a felony under federal law."

Stork's process involved the cutting up of each tool and subjecting it to a chemical analysis by optical emissions. This process analyzes the spectra from an arcing area of the sample. In addition, the Rockwell Hardness C Scale (HRC) was measured at three points on the sample to arrive at an average hardness.

Costs for each test ranged from $50 to $150 per turning tool, a fee that most turners would never consider for a tool costing as little as $6 in some instances. The lab's sampling of steel effectively destroyed the tool.

According to Dr. Jeryl Wright of *Crucible Materials Corporation*, there are no legal definitions of HSS. However, there are American and international standards and definitions. The common understanding of HSS is steel that will resist softening at higher temperatures (usually can withstand a dull red heat, around 1,000˚F) and excellent wear resistance.

More specifically:
*"High-speed steels are high-alloy, tungsten, molybdenum, vanadium, and cobalt bearing steels designed to cut other materials efficiently at high speeds, and must stand up to the extreme heat generated at the tool's cutting edge. This heat can reach 1,000˚F and more depending on cutting conditions, coolants used, and other operational factors."*

## Qualities of HSS

The *Crucible Tool Steel and Specialty Alloy Selector handbook* outlines HSS characteristics for good cutting-tool performance:

- **High attainable hardness**, usually a minimum hardness of HRC 63. Typical metal-cutting tools may be HRC 64–68, depending on grade and application. High carbon

AW 23:2, p52

content, along with elements to promote a more thorough hardening process, are common to all HSS for this purpose.

- **High wear resistance** to promote edge retention during cutting. Constant abrasion wears away tool surfaces. The high volumes of wear-resistant carbides in HSS micro-structures aids in resisting this abrasion.
- **Sufficient impact toughness** to handle interrupted cutting applications, to avoid chipping during cutting, and to avoid breakage in fragile tools. HSS are notably tougher than carbide or ceramic materials.
- **High hardness at elevated temperatures** involves both red hardness (the ability to stay hard at elevated temperature during cutting) and temper resistance (the ability to resist permanent softening over time due to high temperature exposure). The tungsten and/or molybdenum contents promote these properties. When needed, cobalt further enhances red hardness.

## Heat-treating HSS

The heat treating of HSS is an involved process. The *Crucible Tool Steel* handbook referenced also outlines the recommended process for M2 HSS (the most common steel used in English-made tools):

- Preheat to 1,500–1,550°F.
- High-heat to 2,100–2,225°F for 2 to 5 minutes.
- Quench in salt bath or oil to 1,000–1,100°F, then air-cool to hand warm (150°F). Temper immediately.
- Temper at 1,000°F or higher two times for at least two hours. Tempering at 1,025°F yields a 63.5 HRC, while tempering at 1,050°F yields a 62.6 HRC. Both are optimum for maximum toughness and effective stress-relieving.
- Air-cool to room temperature between tempers.

The experts I spoke to believe that the lower-than-normal levels of hardness in some of the samples in the test may have been due to errors in the heat-treating process rather than a conscious choice to make a softer tool. The heat treating of HSS is a most critical part of the toolmaking process—one that must be done precisely and with great care.

## Powders and cryogenics

There are two terms related to turning tools that confuse many turners.

First is the use of *powdered* or *particle metals (PM)*. This is a process in steel making that yields tiny rounded particles rather than a large ingot of steel. The particles are then compressed under heat and high pressure. This process yields a more consistent steel and one with greater

**WOODTURNING TOOL-STEEL ANALYSIS**

| BRAND | COUNTRY OF ORIGIN | CARBON BY % | MANGANESE BY % | PHOSPHORUS BY % | SULFUR BY % | COBALT BY % | SILICON BY % | CHROMIUM BY % | NICKEL BY % | MOLYBDENUM BY % | COPPER BY % | VANADIUM BY % | TUNGSTEN BY % | IRON | HARDNESS (HRC) | PROBABLE STEEL[4] |
|---|---|---|---|---|---|---|---|---|---|---|---|---|---|---|---|---|
| Packard (Hamlet) | UK | 2.30 | 0.00 | 0.00 | 0.00 | 10.70 | 0.77 | 4.00 | 0.00 | 7.10 | 0.00 | 6.60 | 6.50 | B[1] | 68.0 | 2060[5] |
| Sorby | UK | 0.91 | 0.27 | 0.02 | 0.00 | 0.00 | 0.24 | 4.03 | 0.00 | 4.79 | 0.00 | 1.75 | 5.96 | B[1] | 65.0 | M2[6] |
| Apprentice (Craft Supplies) | CHINA | 0.87 | 0.40 | 0.03 | 0.02 | 0.00 | 0.30 | 3.95 | 0.00 | 4.55 | 0.00 | 1.83 | 5.99 | B[1] | 64.0 | M2[6] |
| Benjamin's Best (eBay[2]) | CHINA | 0.85 | 0.35 | 0.02 | 0.02 | 0.02 | 1.18 | 4.50 | 0.07 | 0.29 | 0.11 | 0.12 | 2.41 | B[1] | 65.0 | UN[7] |
| Benjamin's Best (Penn State) | CHINA | 0.86 | 0.62 | 0.03 | 0.02 | 0.05 | 0.36 | 3.91 | 0.11 | 4.73 | 0.15 | 1.93 | 6.34 | B[1] | 58.0 | M2[6] |
| Bodger (Highland Hardware) | CHINA | 1.05 | 0.39 | 0.03 | 0.01 | 0.02 | 0.50 | 4.11 | 0.05 | 0.45 | 0.12 | 0.40 | 2.46 | B[1] | 57.0 | UN[7] |
| Grizzly | CHINA | 0.85 | 0.37 | 0.02 | 0.01 | 0.23 | 0.61 | 4.13 | 0.15 | 2.18 | 0.15 | 0.97 | 4.37 | B[1] | 62.0 | HSS[8] |
| Harbor Freight | CHINA | 0.74 | 0.17 | 0.02 | 0.01 | 0.00 | 0.27 | 4.11 | 0.00 | 0.00 | 0.00 | 1.04 | 17.61 | B[1] | 62.2 | T1[6] |
| Pinnacle (Woodcraft) | CHINA | 0.87 | 0.70 | 0.03 | 0.02 | 0.00 | 0.36 | 4.21 | 0.00 | 4.81 | 0.00 | 2.03 | 6.23 | B[1] | 61.7 | M2[6] |
| Sears Craftsman | CHINA | 0.82 | 0.26 | 0.0 | 0.00 | 0.03 | 0.56 | 4.10 | 0.11 | 3.97 | 0.09 | 0.97 | 0.05 | B[1] | 61.0 | M50[9] |
| Shopsmith[3] | CHINA | 0.94 | 0.11 | 0.02 | 0.01 | 0.09 | 0.22 | 4.02 | 0.11 | 4.50 | 0.14 | 1.68 | 5.84 | B[1] | 64.0 | M2[6] |

1. Balance of tool composition is iron.
2. Purchased new via eBay auction.
3. Part of a 4-piece bowl-turning set (not the standard 5-piece Shopsmith turning set).
4. Interpretations contributed by Stork laboratory technicians, Dr. Jeryl Wright, and Jerry Glaser.
5. 2060 is a particle or powdered metal (PM) HSS with extremely high wear-resistance properties.
6. M2 and T1 are long-established HSS compositions with good track records.
7. Unknown steel. Failed high-speed steel (HSS) test as defined by the American Society for Testing Materials (ASTM). HSS must contain specified amounts of carbon, chromium, vanadium, tungsten, and molybdenum.
8. Meets the minimum amounts to be called an intermediate HSS.
9. M50 is a HSS, primarily used for bearings, but with low-wear resistance.

As a general guideline, high-carbon steel sparks remind some turners of sparklers. At the grinder, you should notice a complex shower of sparks.

As a general guideline, high-speed steel (HSS) sparks remind some turners of tracer bullets and tend to be individual sparks. Note: This test is not always conclusive for HSS.

toughness (a steel's ability to resist breaking under stress or shock).

The other term is *cryogenic treatment* of steel. This is a cold treatment of between 100–300°F below zero. According to Dr. Wright and Jerry Glaser, cryogenic treatment done as a step in the tempering process (after the first temper, but before the second) yields a tool that is more uniform in its heat treating and will offer increased steel toughness.

Some experts question whether cryogenic treatment performed after the heat-treating process produces any improvement in the steel's properties.

## Observations, conclusions

First, beware of generalizations because the test results were for a single tool from the company's inventory. All tools were purchased recently through regular retail catalog channels or new through Internet sales.

Second, let's not forget that a skilled turner can achieve gallery-quality work with any of the tools listed here. With that said, some tools will hold an edge poorly compared to other steels and some will not hold up to heating as low as 525°F (bluing occurs around 570°F).

The more serious problem resides in purchasing tools sold as HSS but are in fact not. If a company spot-checks its supplier and discovers that the tools don't meet HSS standards, it has several choices. It can relabel that shipment, deleting the HSS claim. Or it can refuse the batch, insisting that the supplier correct the problem.

As a turner, I am afraid "buyer beware" does not work with steel content and how well it was heat treated. I may have to use a tool to find out its properties. This is a challenge for the inexperienced turner to judge.

There are some good buys among the legitimate HSS turning tools. And, many tools are a sound choice for someone just entering the world of woodturning.

## Other tool shortcomings

The design adequacy of the tools (shape and thickness of the steel, not the edge profile) is a hard one for the beginner to judge. Some of the tools were lightweights or had designs that were not well thought out. Also, proper heat treating is an unknown.

For consistent and predictable tools, true HSS must be forged and hardened correctly. One of the Sheffield, England, toolmakers reported that his company performs a hardness spot test on each batch of tools delivered from its heat-treating facility. If even one sample doesn't measure up to the company standards, the entire lot is returned to the heat treater.

## Remaining questions

Important questions remain about steel for turners:

- How would each of the steels react to "bluing," which can easily occur at the grinder and even while in use.
- Much has been made about differences of sharpness in steels: Some turners believe high-carbon steel gets sharper than HSS, others believe M2 gets sharper than the high-wear steels such as A11, M4, 2030 and 2060.

*Special thanks for assistance with this test to the late Jerry Glaser, tool maker extraordinaire and AAW Honorary Liftetime Member, and Dr. Jeryl Wright, vice president of Technology for Crucible Materials Corporation and one of the largest makers of specialty tool steels in the USA. Both men are woodturners, so knowledge of both steel and woodturning are special strengths of these two individuals.*

*Alan Lacer (alan@alanlacer.com) is a woodturner, writer, and teacher living near River Falls, WI.*

# Grinder Wheels

*Bill Neddow*

Most people don't realize they might need specialized grinder wheels when they begin their adventure with woodturning. The first thing they think of is usually a lathe. Next, turning tools and wood. Maybe sharpening enters into the process at some point, but grinder wheels? Nobody thinks of them.

Having proper wheels on your grinder makes woodturning simpler and more pleasant than struggling to sharpen tools with improper equipment. Quality wheels that are balanced and suitable for your needs will make sharpening easy. Sharp tools make turning fun.

The old pros can sharpen successfully with just about any grinder and grinder wheel. They probably don't even use a jig to hold the tool at the proper angle. Decades of practice make it easy for them to roll the tool over the grinder wheel by hand and get a perfect edge, whether it is an old gray grinder wheel or the latest ceramic ones.

The rest of us, however, appreciate all the help we can get. When we are starting, it is particularly important to simplify the process and have the most appropriate equipment.

I spent more than a decade as a production turner and used a wide variety of grinder wheels. I have tested all the popular types—and some not so popular. Some wheels work quite well, but I have a cabinet full of wheels that do not. Now I want to share those experiences with you.

## Grinder size and speed

I have used 6" and 8" (15 cm and 20 cm) grinders both high and low speed. Which is best? Probably the one you have. The main difference between the 6" and 8" grinder wheels is the amount of use you get out of them. When a 6" wheel gets down to 5" (13 cm), I generally change the wheel. But I use an 8" wheel until it is about 6", which is a substantial amount of extra grinding. Yes, it costs more to begin with, but you quickly recoup the extra cost. Is it worth buying a new grinder, though? Probably not, unless you are in continual production mode.

More important than the wheel size is the speed of the grinder. There are high-speed (3450 rpm) and low-speed (1725 rpm) grinders. Low-speed grinders are increasingly popular with woodturners because of the lack of heat buildup during use. At a lower speed, there is less chance of *bluing*—heating the metal to a blue color. In the old days, this was considered a terrible thing to do, with good reason. The carbon-steel tools—all we had until the last twenty years—lose their temper if the metal turns blue from heat buildup when grinding. The tools would not hold an edge and had to be ground back significantly to get rid of the soft metal, wasting metal and grinding grit.

The newer high-speed and powdered-metal tools are much less susceptible to overheating, but it can still happen, especially if you put some pressure on the tool and take it beyond the blue stage. Many people recommend dunking a tool in cool water to keep the heat level down. I have done this and seemed to get

AW 26:2, p23

Three aluminum oxide wheels are currently available. The gray one on the left came on a new grinder and is meant for grinding soft steel. The white wheel in the center was also on the grinder and is a little too coarse for woodturners' sharpening needs, but would be suitable for major reshaping of a tool. The blue stone is distributed by Oneway Mfg. and is a type that is designed for woodturners' needs. Note: it is rated for 4,140 rpm, so is meant for a high-speed grinder. Stones are also made specifically for slow-speed grinders.

away with it; however, it can lead to microscopic cracks in the sharp edge. It is better to use a light touch when sharpening a tool to avoid heat in the first place.

If you have a high-speed grinder, there are wheels made specifically for them. Oneway Mfg., for example, sells wheels recommended for use with high-speed grinders. These wheels tend to be harder than the low-speed ones, so don't mix them up. Personally, I prefer the lower-speed wheels because I tend to grind off less of my tool at each sharpening.

## Dressing the wheel

Speed is not the only thing that causes heat. A dull wheel is a major culprit. Dress your wheel as soon as it is not cutting efficiently. When the abrasive particle contacting the steel is sharp, a metal shaving is milled from the steel and ejected. This removes a significant amount of generated heat in a spray of red sparks. A wheel with dull grit ploughs across the steel and transfers much of the heat to the steel. Hard wheels are particularly prone to getting dull.

## Gray wheels

As I mentioned, those who have been turning for quite some time can do a good job of sharpening using the hard gray wheels that normally come with a grinder. For many of these turners, this was all they had, so they learned to live with the grinder wheel's limitations. Gray wheels are designed to stand up to the terrible punishment associated with metalworking shops where thick steel plate is ground, bolts shortened, and other heavy-duty jobs performed. Heavy pressure is usually put on the wheel and the metals are soft. Gray wheels are very hard, so they can do these jobs while lasting a reasonable length of time. They also tend to heat up the metal, which is not a problem in most applications.

We woodturners, however, are performing a light-duty job on very hard tempered steel—simply renewing an edge on an already sharpened tool. The tool's hardness and the resulting heat are our enemy. Gray wheels tend to glaze over easily and stop cutting efficiently. When that happens, the normal reaction is to press harder, increasing the heat. If you have to use a gray wheel, clean it often and use a light touch when grinding.

Ceramic wheels. On the left is a Norton SG wheel and on the right, the 3X wheel. Both cut faster and cooler than aluminum oxide wheels. The SG wheel lasts a very long time. In fact, the wheel on the left has been in daily use for over two years.

## White wheels

White wheels became popular about twenty years ago. They were considered a solution to all of our sharpening problems. And, to a certain extent, they were. They were soft and did not burn hard steel tools as readily. (Most were about an H grade.) The softer the wheel, the less heat buildup.

There was a downside, however. It was easy to wear a groove in a white wheel. As a result, more time was spent dressing the wheels to get rid of grooves, causing most of the wheel to be ground away by the dresser, removing ripples and grooves on the face of the wheel, white powder piling up. The wheels did not last long but did a good job of sharpening. Another problem was that with the quick wear, my grinding jig had to be constantly readjusted in order to maintain the same angles on my tools.

## Blue wheels

After white wheels came blue wheels, which are still popular. They are harder, but not hard enough to cause major problems with overheating the steel. They sharpen tools quickly and easily. They are great workhorses and last longer. I continue to use them. They are a great compromise for light use on hard metals.

## Wheel grit

All these wheels are made from aluminum oxide, the workhorse of the metal industry, and they are relatively inexpensive and do a good job. The blue wheels are the wheels beginners will probably like best. I keep an 80-grit wheel on one side of a grinder and 120 grit on the other side, the first for shaping tools, and the second for creating a fine edge. The edge produced by the 120 grit is sharper than that produced by the 80 grit. It looks almost like a honed edge, yet the edge will not break off the high-speed tools we use, as it used to with carbon-steel tools.

## Ceramic wheels

There are new and interesting wheels on the market. The ones made from a ceramic alumina compound are better than the regular aluminum oxide wheels. The grit on these wheels is not made from your granny's ground-up teapot, even though it is called a ceramic. Each manufacturer closely guards exactly how it produces the material, but basically, the manufacturer converts a colloidal dispersion of hydrosol containing goethite into a semi-solid gel, dries this gel to a glassy state, crushes it to the required grain size, and fires it at between 1200° C and 1600° C. The final product is an abrasive grit of alumina microcrystals.

A major reason why these wheels work so well is that the grits are microcrystalline. This means that each piece of grit is composed of a clump of hundreds of tiny sharp crystals. They continually break away as they are used, exposing millions of fresh sharp cutting edges. These wheels cut cool and leave a fine finish on the tool bevel. By comparison, each piece of aluminum oxide grit is one crystal, which may or may not fracture under pressure and break down to expose smaller edges as they wear. Blunt abrasives rub, which overheats tools.

Ceramic wheels are expensive, but they produce a wonderful edge. I find that when sharpening with 80 grit, the edge looks almost like it was sharpened with a 120-grit wheel. (The finest wheel I can find in ceramic is 80.) They grind almost twice as fast as aluminum oxide (so use a light touch) and produce a keen edge. The wheel self-sharpens as it grinds, it wears slowly, and requires minimal dressing. They can last five times longer than a white wheel, so they are cost-effective.

Because the ceramic is expensive to produce, it is mixed with regular aluminum oxide before being pressed into a wheel. The wheels I am referring to are 50% ceramic, such as the Norton SG wheels sold by many suppliers. Norton also manufactures a wheel that has only a 30% ceramic content, the 3X. While these cut cleanly and run cool, some people have found the wheel wears faster than they would like. Some who have had problems say their wheel has a bond hardness of I. Mine has a bond hardness of K, and has not been a problem. To me, they are good value for money, however, the SG, with its higher ceramic content is well worth the added expense.

Three diamond wheels. On the left is the wheel with 1/8" (3 mm) of diamond/nickel on the rim. The polished spots caused by sharpening high-speed steel are visible. In the center is an unused resin-bonded wheel and on the right (diamond plated) is the one I found most suited to my needs. It started out as an 80-grit wheel and after a year, I am using it as a fine-honing wheel. Note that there is no identification on the two wheels on the right.

## Diamond wheels

Some woodturners use diamond wheels. The theory seems to be that diamond can cut anything. In theory, it does. It is great for cutting ceramics, stone, and aluminum. But diamond wheels do not cut steel efficiently. All the manufacturers agree it should not be used to sharpen the steel we woodturners use—in fact, anything with iron in it. On metals with a ferrous content, the diamond literally disappears.

Diamond particles have a fatal attraction to the iron in the steel. The iron attracts away the carbon in the diamond one atom at a time. The two actually bond at the molecular level, which means a minute amount of the diamond gets carried away with the chip. It sounds like a slow process, and at room temperature it is—thus hand-held diamond honing stones last a long time. Start adding heat, however, and the process speeds up dramatically and catastrophically and you will find a mist of black dust around the base of your grinder, all that is left of your precious diamonds. If you put much pressure on your tool—pushing it into the diamond—you can go through the diamond layer in minutes. If you are gentle, you can get a year or so out of a diamond wheel in use daily, but it will slowly change from an 80-grit wheel to a 120-grit wheel, and eventually will only be good to use as a hone.

I have tried several brands of electroplated diamond wheels, as well as resin-impregnated ones, and an expensive wheel with ⅛" (3 mm) of diamond embedded in nickel around the rim. They all behaved the same way: The diamond quickly wore down to a finer grit and some wheels seemed to need a lot of dressing.

Cleaning them with an old aluminum oxide wheel can restore diamond wheels. That worked on

CBN wheels, my favorites. They cut cleanly, quickly, and smoothly. They have been in continual use for over a year and show no wear.

all wheels I tried, but I was reluctant to use the aluminum oxide on the electroplated wheel—there is only one layer of diamond. In fact, that wheel needed less attention than the other types—just cleaning with WD40.

The wheel with the diamond/nickel mixture wore away the old aluminum oxide grinder wheel faster than my daughter's large cat inhales food. It looked great and cut well after this treatment. What happens is that the aluminum oxide wears away the bonding agent in the diamond wheels, exposing more of the diamond. If I sharpened a few ⅝" (16 mm) gouges on the wheel, however, the surface seemed to deteriorate into a finer grit and the nickel became highly polished. It always looked like it needed cleaning. I eventually took that wheel off the grinder and will give it to a stone carver. That is a $400 loss.

The resin-bonded wheel also lost its edge quickly, but would clean up well with the aluminum oxide dressing stone. The stink of hot resin in the shop was intolerable. That noxious odor was even present when I was sharpening tools. I finally gave the wheel away.

To summarize, the electroplated wheels caused the least amount of trouble. It took about a year to permanently wear them down from 80-grit to honing-wheel condition. The electroplated and resin-coated wheels cost more than $200 apiece, so I do not consider them cost effective.

## CBN wheels

Manufacturers recommend wheels made of CBN—not diamond—for sharpening tool steel. CBN is cubic boron nitride and it is almost as hard a diamond—it will actually scratch diamond. And, it does not have the fatal attraction that diamond has for iron. I have had a pair of these wheels on a grinder for over a year now and can detect no wear. Of course they will eventually wear out, all things do, but the 80-grit is still an 80-grit wheel and the 180 grit is still 180 grit. (I have found I can use the 180-grit wheel to keep my powdered metal tools, like the ones made by Doug Thompson and Dave Schweitzer, sharp as a razor.) The steel is hard enough, yet flexible enough, to maintain a scary-sharp edge, reducing dramatically the need for sanding.

CBN is used widely in industry where precise sharpening and shaping is required. Aircraft manufacturers use distinctively-profiled wheels to sharpen end mills and other precision machining tools to strict tolerances. The CBN sharpening wheels have to perform exactly the same job, with no significant measurable wear, shift after shift, day after day. That is why they last a long time in a woodturning shop.

The CBN wheels I have came prebalanced. I did not have to fuss with dressing and shaping the wheel when it was first mounted. Maintenance of CBN wheels is simple: Scrub them once in a while using a toothbrush and kerosene or WD40. This removes varnish and CA glue that gets transferred from turning tool onto the wheel. I have never had to use aggressive cleaning techniques on these wheels.

If I use a CBN wheel, I never have to adjust my sharpening jig. I can leave it set exactly the way I want, and since the wheel never gets smaller, I get the same grind every time. One light pass over the 180-grit wheel is enough to sharpen a tool to razor-blade quality most of the time. If my tool is really dull, then one pass over the 80 grit wheel, followed by a light pass over the 180 grit wheel will return the edge to perfection.

CBN grinder wheels come in almost any shape desired. The choice is endless . . . except for simple bench grinder wheels. (The shape of a standard bench grinder wheel is generally called 1A1 for diamond/CBN.) Bench grinder wheels are available, but you have to search for them. Check with your local metalworking shops.

I intend for this brief survey of grinder wheels to accomplish three objectives. First, to provide information to help you buy grinder wheels with more confidence. Second, to make your turning experience more pleasurable. And third, to help you save money—I know—I have spent far too much on grinder wheels over the years. It is my own fault, of course, but I am too curious for my own good!

*Bill Neddow spends his retirement creating bowls for galleries and taking part in studio tours. He also does some demonstrating. Bill considers himself a semiproduction turner, following themes in his bowl designs, but trying something different with each one. He is fascinated not only by how to do something but why it works, a byproduct of thirty years as a writer, editor, and publications manager. He lives in Ottawa, Canada, with his wife and about 3,500 dry rough-turned bowls. His website is billneddow.com. You can email him at bill.neddow@sympatico.ca.*

# Identifying Grinder Wheels

Most manufacturers use a system for identifying grinder wheels. There are variations—a number of manufacturers modify the identification system to meet their needs, and not all use the complete sequence of identifying codes. Some wheels carry an absolute minimum of information. It is possible, however, to figure out the code on most wheels.

There are two systems, quite similar. One is for identifying bonded wheels (made of such substances as aluminum oxide and silicone carbide). The other is for diamond and CBN (superabrasive) wheels.

I have tried to simplify the systems to cover only the types of wheels woodturners generally use.

### Identifying a Bonded Wheel

**Number and Letter Sequence**

| | |
|---|---|
| Prefix | 51 |
| Abrasive Type | A |
| Abrasive Grain Size | 80 |
| Grade (Hardness) | K |
| Structure | 5 |
| Bond Type | V |
| Manufacturer's Record | 05 |

*Prefix:* Manufacturers' symbols indicating the exact kind of abrasive. This is optional, and often manufacturers do not use it.

*Abrasive Type:* Identifies the primary grain used to make the wheel.

| | |
|---|---|
| A | Regular Aluminum Oxide |
| WA | White Aluminum Oxide |
| Z | Aluminum Zirconium |
| C | Silicone Carbide |
| SG | Seeded Gel (Ceramic) |

*Abrasive Grain Size:* Indicates the size of grit particles going through a screen. For example, 80 grit is what goes through one row of screen with 80 wires in one linear inch. 120 grit means there are 120 lines of screen, making the size of the grit going through a 1" (25 mm) linear line of screen smaller. The measurements range from coarse to very fine. I have found that woodturners use the medium-grit range (46, 54, 60) and fine (70, 80, 90, 100, 120, 150, 180). We most commonly use 46 grit for shaping a tool and 80 grit for sharpening. Some turners use a finer-grit wheel to keep the tool sharp, such as 120 grit.

*Grade (Hardness):* Hardness is rated from A to Z with A being the weakest bond and Z being the strongest. A weaker bond is preferred for grinding harder materials like tool steel. Most of the wheels we use are in the I to K range. An increase in the hardness grade by one or two letters can make a dramatic difference. A move from an H to an I, for example, could double the life of the wheel.

*Structure:* Basically the spacing between abrasive grains, represented by a series of numbers, with the structure becoming more open as the number increases. A 1 would be very dense. We are after a more open structure, which would probably be 5 or above.

*Bond Type:* The most common bond types are vitrified V and resin B. Vitrified is basically a vitreous glass much like pottery or glassware fired in a kiln, which is why there is such a fuss about not using a chipped or dropped stone made with this material—it may be cracked and can blow up. Resin is more commonly found in cut-off wheels, but can also be found in diamond and CBN wheels. There are other bond types such as Rubber R and Silicate S.

*Manufacturer's Record:* A private manufacturer's marking to identify a wheel. The use is optional.

### Identifying a Superabrasive Wheel

The marking system for superabrasive grinder wheels is somewhat different.

**Number and Letter Sequence**

| | |
|---|---|
| Abrasive Type | D |
| Abrasive Grain Size | 80 |
| Grade (Hardness) | N |
| Concentration | 100 |
| Bond Type | M |
| Bond Modification | 77 |
| Abrasive Depth | ⊠ |
| Manufacturer's Record | 4 |

*Abrasive Type:* The letter D indicates that the abrasive is diamond. The letter B or CB is used for CBN.

*Abrasive Grain Size:* The number 80 represents the average grain size fitting through a linear inch of wire mesh (e.g., 120 grit would mean 120 lines of mesh).

*Grade (Hardness):* Like conventional wheels the letter N identifies the hardness of the wheel. Resin- and metal-bonded wheels, however, are produced with almost no porosity and the grade of the wheel is controlled by modifying the bond formulation.

*Concentration:* The number 100 is known as a concentration number, indicating the amount of diamond abrasive contained in the mix in the wheel. The number 100 corresponds to an abrasive content of 25 percent by volume. For CBN wheels, the number represents a concentration of 24 percent by volume. Concentration numbers of 75 or higher are are preferred. For CBN wheels, Norton drops the concentration section. Norton refers to the concentration as the grade and uses the letter W for 100 concentration, T for 75 concentration and Q for 50 concentration.

*Bond Type:* The letter M or N indicates the bond is metallic. Another bond is resin, represented by the letter B or R. There are also vitrified wheels V.

*Bond Modification:* This is the manufacturer's notation of any special bond type or modification. It is optional information.

*Abrasive Depth:* The working depth of the abrasive section, generally measured in inches. For example: ⅛" (3 mm). This is very important in determining the life of the wheel and its initial cost. A bond layer of ⅛" provides about half the life of a bond layer 1/4" (6 mm) thick.

*Manufacturer's Record:* As with the bonded wheels, this is optional information on the manufacturer's private identification code for the wheel.

**Safety Note**

Grinder wheels can explode as they rotate at high speed. It is absolutely necessary to wear an impact-resistant faceshield when using a grinder.

# Comparing Sharpening Alternatives

*Jim Echter*

One of the major differences between an expert turner and most beginners is how sharp each turner keeps his tools.

Sharp tools are also are why one beginner becomes proficient much faster than another, and dull tools probably discourage some beginners who just give up. Our turning tools really are consumable items just like sandpaper. They need to be sharpened much more frequently than many beginners imagine, and yes, repeated sharpening does use them up although it may take years.

When I teach I always advise beginning and intermediate turners to spend time learning how to properly sharpen their tools. A key advantage of belonging to the AAW and becoming active in your local chapter is that our clubs offer many opportunities to learn how to sharpen properly. My local chapter conducts sharpening workshops and we also have a mentoring program to help our new members get their tools properly sharpened so they have one less barrier to learning.

This article provides an overview of the various sharpening systems currently available: dry grinders, wet grinders, belt systems, and the new rotary see-through grinders that have come to market in recent years. I will explain the primary features, benefits, disadvantages, and costs of each system. Because many turners also have other woodworking interests, we will also look at other possible uses. Everyone has a different budget and workshop setup, so there is no single perfect solution, system, or method for sharpening.

## Dry grinders

The standard in most woodturning shops is a bench grinder with two 8" × 1" (200 mm × 25 mm) aluminum oxide wheels. Aluminum oxide wheels, usually colored white, blue, or pink, cut faster and cooler than grey carborundum wheels. Occasionally you can find a price near $100 on an 8" slow-speed (1700–1800 rpm) or dual-speed (1700–1800 and 3400–3600 rpm) grinder with white wheels, which is a great deal. Some of these machines may have a small water tray for cooling the tool tip; the wheel itself runs dry.

For everyday sharpening, many woodturners rely on a slow-speed grinder with two 8" × 1" white aluminum oxide wheels. On Jim Echter's machine, the left wheel has a TruGrind jig for sharpening gouges, skews, and parting tools. The right has a Veritas adjustable-angle platform for sharpening scrapers.

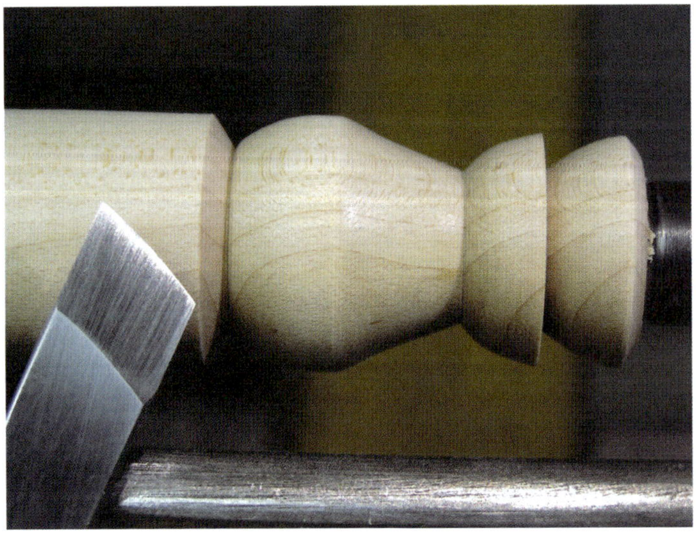

Here's why: with sharp tools, you can turn cleanly and skip directly to your finest sandpaper grit.

AW27:5, p27

| Dry grinders | | | | |
|---|---|---|---|---|
| Manufacturer | Model | Details | Cost | Web address |
|  Baldor Industrial Grinder | 8250W | 8", 3600 rpm, replace grey wheels with aluminum oxide wheels | $900 | baldor.com |
|  Delta Variable Speed Grinder | 23-199 | 8", 1725 and 3450 rpm, one 60-grit aluminum oxide and one 36-grit grey wheel | $150 | deltamachinery.com |
|  Grizzly Heavy-Duty Bench Grinder | G0596 | 8", 1800 rpm, replace grey wheels with aluminum oxide wheels | $495 | grizzly.com |
|  Woodcraft Slow Speed Grinder | 105780 | 8", 1700 rpm, comes with 60-grit and 120-grit aluminum oxide wheels | $125 | woodcraft.com |

The 8" grinder solution is generally considered fast at both reshaping tool profiles and putting new edges on your tools. That is why you are likely to find one in most woodturners' shops, woodturning schools, and at most clubs. If you learn how to use the 8" grinder, you will be comfortable when you take a class, visit other turners' shops, if you teach, or if you mentor beginners. The 8" grinder has two disadvantages: first, with carbon-steel tools it is easy to overheat (blue) the metal and draw its temper; and second, the standard toolrest leaves much to be desired when you are trying to shape a gouge or a skew chisel. Many beginners have carbon-steel tools because they inherited them with their lathe or they bought them at a garage sale. There is much less risk of overheating modern high-speed steel tools, a big advantage for turners who sharpen often.

Interestingly, when a representative from a major abrasives company visited our local club, he made the point that a 3600-rpm grinder with proper wheels was actually cooler on the steel than the same wheel running at 1800 rpm. The rep explained that the wheel surface was designed to fracture and expose fresh cutting edges at the higher speed. I think the higher speed would be an advantage for a professional tool-and-die maker who works with metal every day. However, most woodturners find that slow-speed grinders are easier to control, which is why they have become so prevalent in our shops. *Dry grinders* lists major and popular brands of dry grinders.

While dry grinders are fast and great for reshaping a tool, they do leave a ragged burr on the edge that sometimes needs honing, especially on fine detail tools like the skew chisel. Some production bowl turners prefer the edge right off the grinder because they believe its raggedness is like a serrated knife cutting through bread, especially when roughing green blanks. Some turners use a buffing wheel to hone their tools, while others prefer to touch them up with sharpening stones.

Dry grinders generally do not come with much in the way of toolrests. While you could cobble up your own, I believe you will get best results with aftermarket grinding jigs and platform rests designed for sharpening turning tools. Good jigs and platforms help you maintain the tool's shape and bevel angle every time you sharpen. Gouges are particularly difficult to sharpen freehand, but inventors and manufacturers have come up with a number of clever jigs to help you grind and maintain the correct shape and angle. Adjustable-angle platform rests help sharpen skews, parting tools, and scrapers.

Recent and noteworthy jig innovations include the Hannes Tool multipivot gouge jig that permits the multiangle grind advocated by the hat-turner JoHannes Michelsen, and a heavy-duty angle gauge and adjustable-angle platform designed by Stuart Batty of Boulder, Colorado.

## Wet grinders

Wet grinders generally feature a 10" × 2" (25 cm x 5 cm) wheel turning slowly in a water bath. The water

## Grinding jigs and platforms

| Manufacturer | Model | Details | Cost | Web address |
|---|---|---|---|---|
| 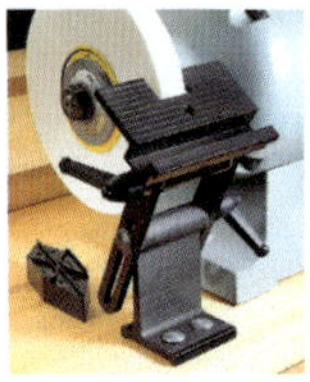 Lee Valley Veritas Grinder Tool Rest | 05M23.01 | Platform rest | $55 | veritastools.com |
| Lee Valley Veritas Skew-Grinding Jig | 05N13.01 | Jig for skews, use with platform rest | $30 | veritastools.com |
|  Oneway Wolverine Grinding Jig | 2291 | Base, sliding arm and platform rest | $90 | oneway.ca |
| Oneway Wolverine Vari-Grind Attachment | 2480 | Jig for gouges, use with platform rest | $55 | oneway.ca |
|  PSI Woodworking Complete 4-Piece Precision Lathe Chisel Sharpening System | LCGRIND4 | Platform with jigs for gouge and skew | $115 | pennstateind.com |
|  Sharp-Fast Tool Guide System | S900 | Jig for gouges | $125 | tmiproducts.net |
|  Robert Sorby Universal Sharpening System | 447-RS | Platform with jigs for gouge and skew | $140 | robert-sorby.co.uk |
| 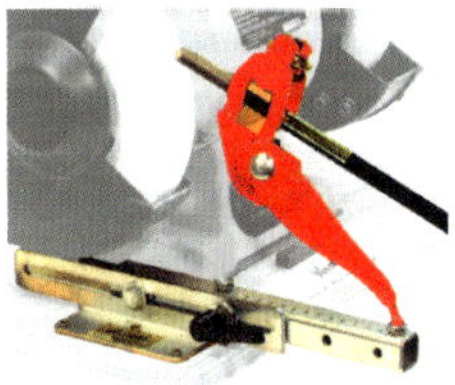 Tru-Grind Sharpening System | TRUGR | Platform with jigs for gouge and skew | $130 | woodcut-tools.com |
|  Hannes Tool Vector Grind Fixture | | Jig for gouges; multibevel grind | $140 | hannestool.com |
| SB Tools Angle Gauges | | Three gauges for setting grinder platform angles | $105 | woodturning.org |

both cools the steel and carries away the grinding waste. Wet grinders can produce a very fine, smooth, and polished edge, by far the finest edge of all the different mechanical sharpening systems. Many turners believe there is an advantage to having such a sharp edge, but many other turners believe it is just not worth the expense for our type of woodworking. Beliefs aside, the real advantage of a wet grinder is that it is nearly impossible to overheat the tool edge, no matter how thin you grind it.

The most widely known wet-grinding system is the Tormek T-7. Tormek offers an accessory kit for sharpening woodturning tools. JET Tools introduced their version a few years ago, also with accessories for turning tools. Lately there have been some inexpensive wet grinders coming out of the Far East, although these typically do not have a jig or accessory kit for woodturning tools.

One argument that many turners have against wet grinders is that they do not want a water tray near the lathe because it fills up with chips and makes a mess. Vendors have responded with nice covers to help keep debris out of the water, but many turners still consider it a hassle to have to uncover and cover the unit every time they sharpen. The other issue is that compared to a dry grinder, a wet system is considered slow when initially shaping a tool profile. Before Tormek came out with their woodturning accessory kit, many turners felt that system also was too slow. However, in my opinion, the jigs available today make sharpening turning tools on a wet system very comparable in speed to sharpening with a dry grinder.

Wet systems are quite expensive, especially when you add in the cost of the accessory kits. On the other hand, most wet-grinding machines include a leather honing wheel, so they do offer a complete solution. If you are a carver or if you use hand planes and chisels for flat work, then it will be easier to justify the expense of one of these systems.

**Wet grinders**

| Manufacturer | Model | Details | Cost | Web address |
|---|---|---|---|---|
|  Grizzly Wet Grinder | T10010 | 10" wet wheel, leather honing wheel | $170 | grizzly.com |
| Grizzly Accessory Kit #2 | T10024 | Wheel dresser, angle guide, tool holder. | $55 | grizzly.com |
|  Harbor Freight Wet/Dry Grinder | 35098 | Both an 8" wet and 6" dry grinder, no accessories available | $65 | harborfreight.com |
|  JET Slow Speed Wet Sharpener | JSSG-10 | 10" wet wheel, variable speed, leather honing wheel | $350 | jettools.com |
| 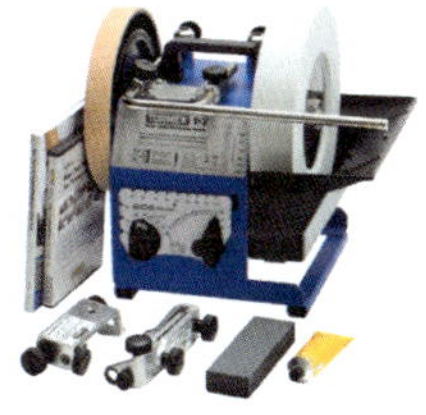 Tormek Sharpener | T-7 | 10" wet wheel, leather honing wheel | $630 | tormek.com |
| Tormek Woodturner's Kit | TNT-708 | Toolrest, gouge jig, honing wheel, angle guide | $320 | tormek.com |

## Belt sharpeners

A belt sander offers another way of sharpening turning tools. Most belt-sander systems produce a flat edge, instead of the hollow-ground edge that comes from wet and dry grinders. Some turners make the case that the flat edge gives them better control at the lathe. Others believe that a hollow-ground edge makes for easier honing, and therefore is sharper. What I find interesting is that tool vendors and knife makers all use belt systems in their manufacturing processes. Today, one can purchase high-quality fine-grit belts impregnated with aluminum oxide, blue zirconia, or silicon carbide. These belts are designed to produce a mirror finish on high-speed steel tools. This makes belt systems possibly the best all-around solution for a sharpening system.

The case for belt systems includes: (1) they are cooler than grinding wheels because the belts dissipate heat better; (2) since the belt usually is running away from the edge, you cannot jam the tool like you can with a grinding wheel; and (3) belts are easy to change. You can switch from a coarse belt for profiling to a fine belt for sharpening in a couple of seconds. If the belt is worn out, it is quick to replace. Belts are consistent and do not change dimensionally, like grinding wheels, and belts do not need to be dressed like wheels. Some belt systems, like most wet grinders, have the additional advantage of a buffing or honing wheel, which gives better and more consistent results than honing by hand.

The British tool manufacturer Robert Sorby has recently introduced their ProEdge Sharpening System. It has several optional accessories that include jigs for gouges and skews plus a honing wheel; these are included in the Pro-Edge Plus system. What I find interesting is that the belt runs toward the tool edge, whereas other systems have the belt running away from the edge so it cannot catch and tear, which seems safer. The ProEdge can do this because its various jigs position the tools in a repeatable manner. However, one major disadvantage of the Sorby system is that it uses nonstandard belts.

One of our industry's long-time advocates of belt sharpening is professional turner Jon Siegel of Wilmot, NH. Jon makes a strong case for the flat sanding belt plus honing wheels. Jon had developed and sold a well-thought-out sharpening system based on an inexpensive imported belt sander and buffing wheel. In my opinion, Jon's Big Tree Sharpening System should have been on everyone's tool evaluation and purchase lists. Jon's company recently suspended manufacturing this system, but a redesign is in the works and it will probably be available again. Meanwhile, I decided to build my own belt sharpening system based on one of these low-cost import sanders, presented elsewhere in this collection. If you are a woodturner, the chances are good that you are frugal and handy and could build yourself a system if you wanted.

**Belt sharpeners**

| Manufacturer | Model | Details | Cost | Web address |
|---|---|---|---|---|
|  Harbor Freight Combination Belt/Disc Sander | 97181 | 4" × 36" belt with 6" disk sander | $100 | harborfreight.com |
|  Kalamazoo Belt/Wheel Sander | 2SK7 | 2" × 48" belt with 7" grinding wheel | $660 | kalamazooind.com |
|  Lee Valley Sander/Grinder | 68Z75.01 | 1" belt grinder, no motor | $90 | leevalley.com |
|  Robert Sorby ProEdge Plus System | PED01 | 2" belt system with jigs for turning tools and honing accessories | $550 | robert-sorby.co.uk |

## Rotary see-through grinders

Recently, two companies, Jooltool and Work Sharp, have released affordable rotary grinders into the marketplace, alongside the unusual VisiGrind machine. These sharpening systems have a horizontal wheel or sharpening disk and you sharpen the tool on the bottom of the wheel, not on the top like horizontal water wheels. The unique feature is that the disks are slotted or perforated so you can actually observe the tool tip as it is being sharpened. The Work Sharp machine features interchangeable disks and a sanding-belt attachment, and the company recently has introduced a tool bar attachment that accepts Tormek and JET jigs for turning tools. All three manufacturers say their systems run much cooler than conventional sharpening equipment.

It is amazing to use one of these systems and actually see the edge being ground. I think for the experienced and professional turner who has great tool control, using one of these freehand rotary sharpening systems may be very quick for edge touchups. A new turner might find it difficult to use one of these systems freehand or to reshape a new tool. For that reason, the Work Sharp 3000 with JET or Tormek jigs for turning tools might be an interesting though expensive choice.

**Rotary see-through grinders**

| Manufacturer | Model | Details | Cost | Web address |
|---|---|---|---|---|
|  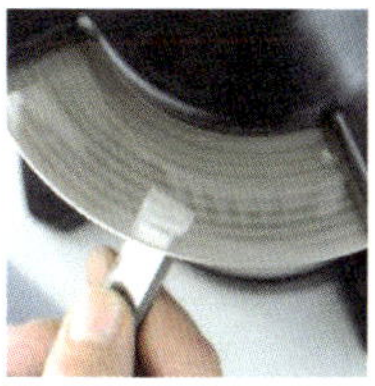 Clear-View VisiGrind | K-SM180 | See-through perforated diamond disk, top-view magnifier | $800 | sharperdrills.com |
|  Jooltool | Intro Pack | 3M Ninja See-Thru abrasive disks | $300 | jooltool.com |
|  Work Sharp | 3000 | See-through dry grinder that can be used top side or see-through from below. Tool bar attachment accepts turning-tool jigs. | $300 | worksharptools.com |

## Summary

As in most things in life, there are multiple methods for solving the woodturner's sharpening needs. You can get a sharp edge with any of these: a dry grinder, a wet grinder, a belt sharpener, or a rotary sharpener. It depends on your budget, your time, and whether you want to sharpen other nonturning tools. If you are a beginner, attend a sharpening workshop or class, and try out different systems. Pick one and go for it. Whatever system you choose, you will need to practice using it. The important thing to remember is that you need to touch up the edge of your turning tools before they get dull, so you can experience the joy of always turning with sharp tools.

---

*Jim Echter is a professional turner who lives near Rochester, NY. He specializes in making tools for fiber artists, turning custom architectural pieces, and teaching. Jim's home club is the Finger Lakes Woodturners Association, and his website is truecreations.biz.*

*Note: Prices current 2012—2013*

# Improving a Grinder

*Bob Vaughan*

I bought a second-or-third-hand Baldor 7in., 3600 RPM bench grinder not long ago. It had more cast iron than my new Baldor grinders, and after a little motor work, it ran quite smoothly. I knew that it would make a great low-risk platform for some modifications that I have had in mind for making a good grinder better. I felt that with a little time and effort, and minimal investment of cash, I could make this grinder safer, easier, and faster to use.

I ended up making seven modifications:

1. Tool tray on top of grinder.
2. Electrical outlet under tool tray.
3. Larger tool rests and tool rest posts.
4. Custom overlay plates for tool rests.
5. Quick adjust handles, instead of bolts, on the tool rest post and rest.
6. Larger eye shields.
7. Wing nuts to hold outside wheel guards, instead of bolts.

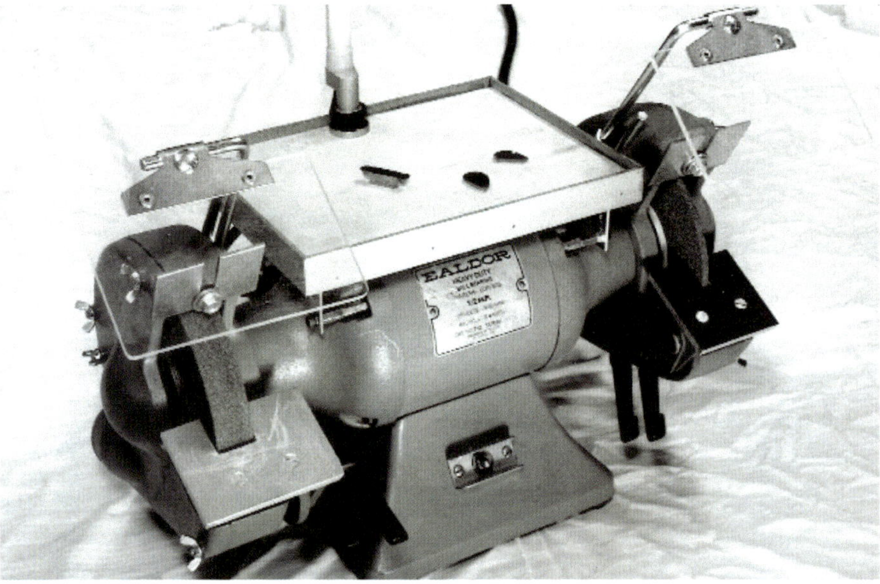

The author's souped up grinder, ready to use with new tool rests, tray and other accoutrements. Photo by Bob Vaughan.

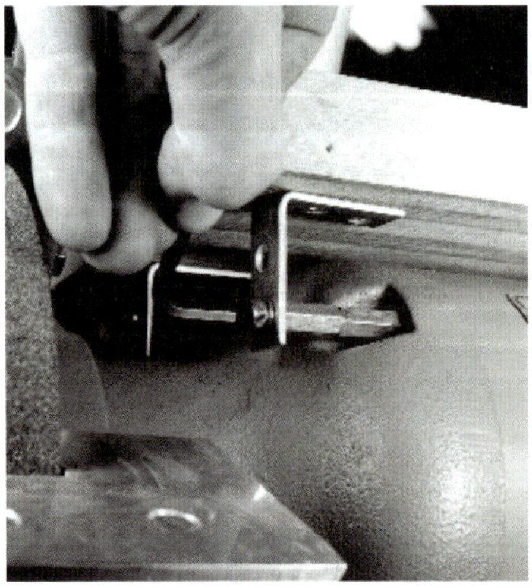

An Allen wrench tightens the shelf mounting bracket. Allen head works well in tight space.

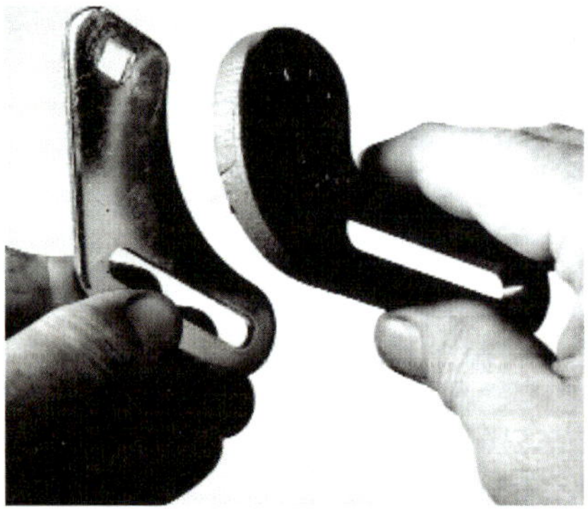

Cast iron tool rest holder is much heavier than the stamped steel ones originally on the author's grinder.

## The tool tray

I wanted a convenient, out-of-the -way place to put tools, cutters, dressers, and other items that normally litter the grinding area. I also wanted a platform that would accommodate an electrical outlet and a gooseneck light. So my first objective was to mount an 8 in. x 11 in. x 3/4 in. thick plywood tool tray on top of the machine. Plywood was fine since I wouldn't put a water pot up there and risk spillage down over the motor and switch. A 1/8 in.-thick x 1 in.-wide edge was added to keep stuff from vibrating off.

First, I removed the wheel, flanges and both wheel guards so that only the grinder's motor itself was left. Next, I did some measuring. I found that I had to replace the two top motor bolts with two lengths of 10-24 threaded rod and rod coupling nuts. Because of the curve of the motor's end bells, I had to use two

AW 14:1, p22

rod coupling nuts to get enough extension to mount the steel angle brackets. The threaded rod was cut so that there was just enough rod for the second nut to hold securely yet leave enough internal thread for the angle bracket's mounting screw.

I mounted the angle brackets to the threaded couplings, positioned the tray, and marked the bottom of the tray to indicate the angle bracket's wood-screw holes. Then I removed the angle brackets from the threaded rod coupling nuts and screwed them to the bottom of the plywood tray. Next, I mounted the tray to the grinder. I positioned the tray toward the rear of the grinder so it wouldn't create a shadow or interfere with grinding activities.

I wired and mounted a grounded electrical outlet under the back overhang of the tray. I wired the grinder's switch directly to this outlet. Now I have a place to plug in my overhead gooseneck light and other things as needed.

The author holds the old motor bolt in front of the mounting bracket, which already has all-thread and one coupling nut installed. The second coupler is needed to install the angle bracket.

## Tool rest modifications

I quickly realized that the stamped steel tool rests that came with this lower-priced grinder were not rigid enough for my needs. I ordered the cast iron ones that are standard on the deluxe 7-in. versions. Instead of installing the standard 1/4 bolts and nuts to hold my tool rest and post, I ordered quick-adjusting handles with a 5/16 inch thread. I thought that the original 1/4-in. thread was a little flimsy for these handles. Now I don't have to go on a wrench hunt every time I need to adjust the angle of the tool rest.

For this thread size upgrade, the tool rest posts had to filed out to accept the 5/16-in. thread. Next, the tool rest post and the inner grinding wheel guard had to be drilled and tapped for the larger 5/16-18 thread.

The small surface of the standard cast iron tool rest wouldn't allow me the safety and convenience I wanted for my grinding chores. I decided to mount an overlay plate on top of the tool rest and custom fit each overlay plate to my various grinding wheels. If I have to grind something with a short bearing surface, I can simply remove the plate.

I first mounted the tool rest and a grinding wheel to determine how the inside of the grinding wheel relates to the tool rest. I then marked the top of the tool rest and drilled and tapped the surface of the tool rest with two 10-32 holes about 1-1/2 in. apart. I put in a good countersink to compensate for potential protruding of the flat-head screws. I then cut out some 3x3 and 3x4 plates from some scrap 1/4-inch thick aluminum. They were aligned on the tool rest against the wheel and marked for the mounting holes. I then drilled a clearance hole and countersunk so a flat-head screw would go below the surface of the tool rest plate.

Tool rest plates were made for 1/4in. wheels, 1-in. wheels, and a cut-off wheel. I quickly found that aluminum wasn't the best material, so I'm in the process of getting them made out of 1/4-in. steel plate. Aluminum will do for a while, though.

I used my regular wood-cutting handsaw with an old blade to cut the aluminum. Feeding very slowly (1 in. per 15 seconds), it did an acceptable job, but it did throw aluminum chips everywhere.

Now I can safely profile grind around the sides of cutter bits or use a cut-off wheel with ease and safety.

## Other modifications

The standard GA-10 eye shields that came with this model grinder were OK, but I opted for ordering the larger GA-11 type (standard on Baldor's Deluxe 7 in. models.) They have a thicker steel rod and wider eye protection area. Again, I had to re-tap a 1/4-20 hole for a 5/16-18 thread in the inside wheel guard for the more secure mounting. Now I can clamp on a magnifying glass and not worry about movement caused by vibration.

Because I change grinding wheels a lot, I decided to get around the wrench-and-bolt ceremony with the outside wheel guards. I got some 1/4-20 threaded rod and some wing nuts. The rod was cut into short

A file is used to open up the adjusting slot in the tool rest support. Also shown is the newly enlarged and threaded hole for the tool rest.

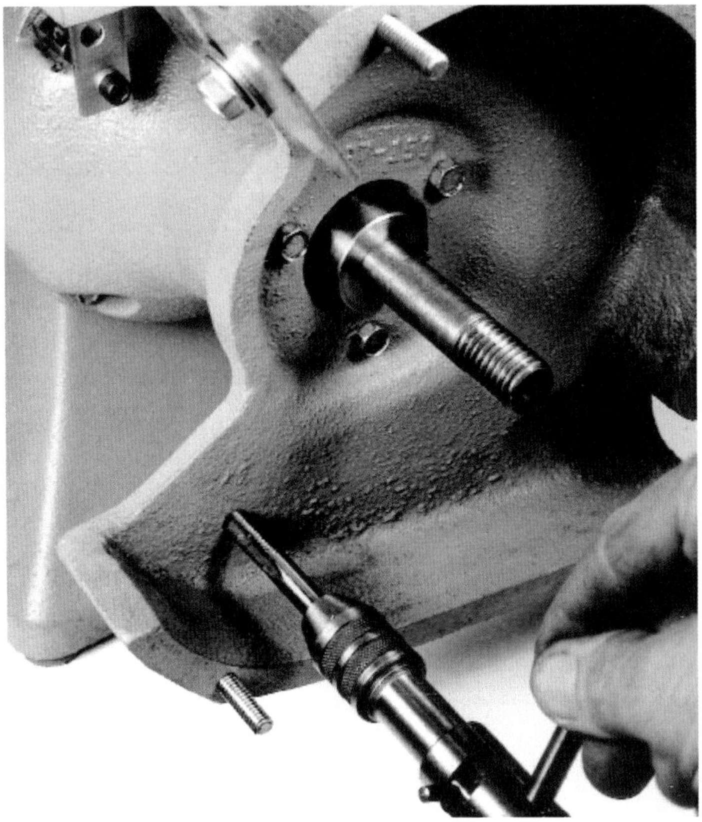

A hand tap is used to thread the inside wheel guard for quick adjust handles. The stud shown is for mounting the outside wheel guard

pieces so that enough protruded to accepted a wing nut. Now, the only wrench I need is one for the grinding wheel. True, there are some slip-on arbor nuts available, but I haven't gotten into that yet. I suspect they won't hold as securely as standard arbor nuts.

## Tips

First activity: Read this article to the end before you get the hardware. The grinder will have to be partially disassembled, so plan ahead to avoid unnecessary activity.

Determine your top tray dimensions before disassembly, taking into consideration overhang and interference with shadow, wheel guards, and tool sharpening processing.

And, as with any machine modification, be careful. Don't try any of this with the machine plugged in; if you are unsure how to do something, seek competent help. Don't be intimidated by the rudimentary metalwork mentioned herein. If you're unfamiliar with drilling, tapping and filing metal, know that it's merely a matter of learning a few simple rules and there is a wealth of good information available on the Internet and at the public library. There might be a recreational metalworker or machinist in your own neighborhood that could help.

Why doesn't the factory offer these options? My guess is that they wouldn't stay competitive. Also, things, like the locking handles and wing nuts holding on the outside wheel guards wouldn't be at all appropriate for industrial situations where people of diverse skill levels are using the same grinder. For woodturners, the user and the owner will be the same, so the degree of care will be higher.

Now that I've had a while to enjoy the benefits of these modifications, the long-term payback in speed, convenience, and safety was well worth the effort.

*Bob Vaughan is an amateur turner who makes his living rebuilding woodworking machinery in Roanoke, VA.*

# Jigs Grind Consistent Edges

*Kirk Deheer*

I've been fortunate enough to meet many of the world's best-known woodturners when they've passed through Provo. Because I'm a self-proclaimed tool freak, I've examined their tools and watched their every move at the lathe.

Most of the turners I've met are freehand sharpeners, as I was when I started assisting them at workshops and demonstrations.

That all changed when Dale Nish asked me to assist him in a beginner's class. Because Dale is a freehand sharpener, he asked me to demonstrate sharpening jigs. And he gave me 30 minutes' notice!

Oh my gosh—that was all new to me. I could quickly see that the bowl gouge would be the hardest tool to sharpen with a jig. So I grabbed my bowl gouge and started to set up the jig.

As I remember, the demonstration went well, but there were questions from the class. Many of them had tried to follow the instructions that accompanied the jig, but my setup wasn't anything like their instruction sheets recommended.

## Adjust your thinking

As I researched sharpening jigs, I realized that the control leg did not set the bevel angle like I thought but adjusted the *angle* of the grind on the gouge wing.

The first major hurdle is that the instructions packaged with the Wolverine jig and similar systems confuse new woodturners and experienced turners alike. The side grind is not the *length* of the wing (how far the grinding extended), as the packaged instructions lead you to believe. Rather, the side grind is the *angle* at which the wing is ground.

Although the great turners have different preferences for the bevel angle, there is one common denominator: The bevel of the tool follows around the side to the wing. Unfortunately, if you follow the directions packaged with the sharpening jigs, the wing angles are much steeper than the nose angle. It's no wonder great instructors direct students away from sharpening jigs.

## What goes wrong

I bet this has happened to you: You introduce a straight and extremely steep side grind to the work without any support (steel in contact with wood), and the piece grabs the wing and pulls it into the wood. Almost instantly, the gouge rolls over, allowing the edge to dig deeper into the wood and "Bang!" Another catch. Then you put the tool on the shelf because it's hard to control.

Don't quit—there's a way to get comfortable with grinding your turning tools—and a better way to grind your gouges.

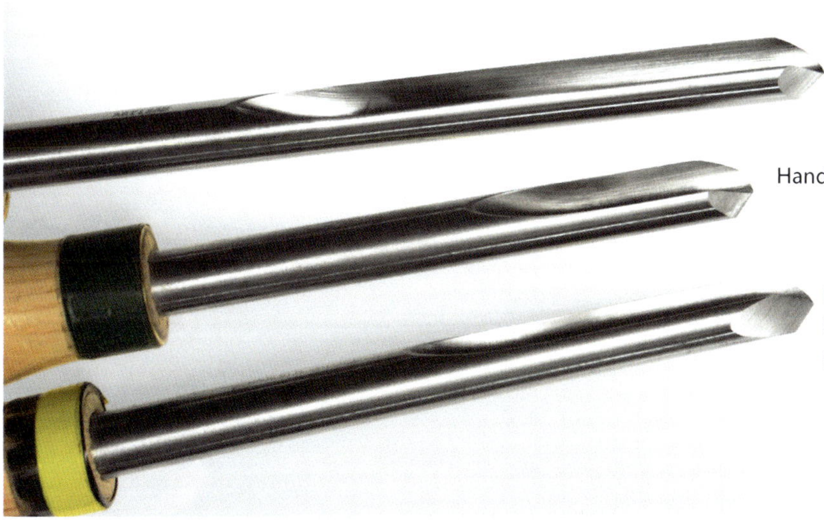


Photos: John Hetherington Illustrations: Roxanne LeMoine

AW 21:4, p32

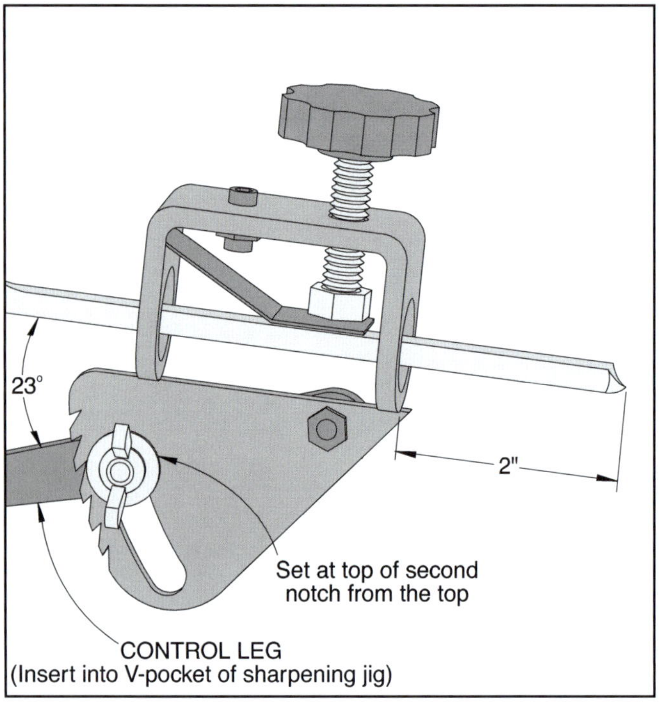


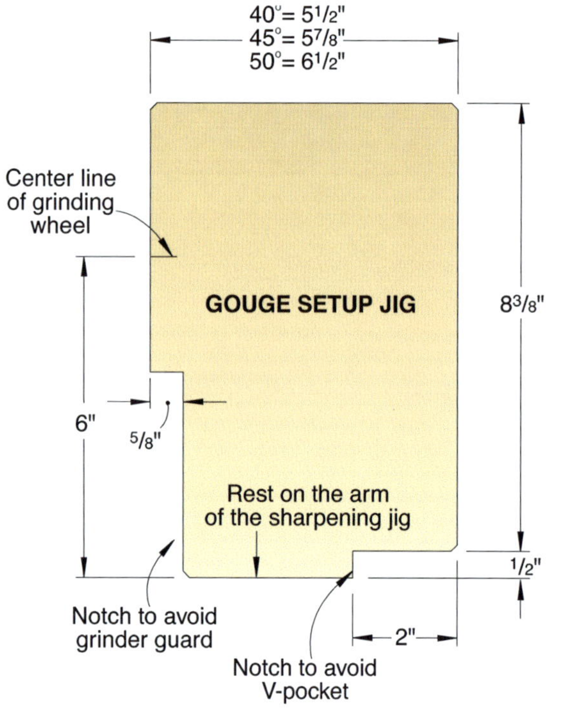


To be sure, freehand grinding is faster. But until you acquire keen grinding skills, the method I'll outline here will help you reduce the variables at the grinder and help you produce a wing (side grind) that matches the nose.

The process works with all of the popular sharpening jigs I've found on the market, including the Wolverine sharpening jig and the Tru-Grind jig.

## A proven method

Place the flute of the gouge against your grinding wheel and get the shape (profile) that you want. Remember that a straight edge on your flute is more aggressive than a curved edge (convex), which is less agressive and easier to control.

Now you're ready to set the control leg on the tool holder. The farther you move the control leg forward (toward the wheel), the more side grind you remove and the steeper the angle. The farther back you move the control leg (away from the wheel), the less side grind you remove.

This was the hardest concept for me to grasp and is how most woodturners stray off course with sharpening jigs.

## Set the side grind

I believe the control leg should be set at 23 degrees from the bottom of the gouge flute to the top of the second notch on the Wolverine Vari-Grind jig, as shown. You can set this angle and never have to move it again.

Now, slide your gouge into the jig, as shown. To quickly set the jig to 2", use the notch on the Gouge Setup Jig, shown here, or mount a 2" set block on your grinder base.

This 2" setting is key so you can get consistent sharpening. If your control leg and the length of the tool are the same, you've set two sides of a triangle. You're on your way! Now you just need to set the third side (the cutting edge) and sharpen without wasting time or steel.

## Set the bevel angle

To set the bevel angle, make a **Gouge Setup Jig** from ¾" plywood, as shown in the drawing. Then use this jig to set the V-arm at the proper distance from the wheel (6" from the V-pocket to the centerline of the wheel), as shown in *Photo 1*. You may have to elevate your grinder. You can rely on this jig regardless of the size of your gouge or the diameter of your grinding wheel.

The setup jig quickly locks your grinding into a consistent bevel angle. You may wish to make three of these jigs—one each for 40, 45, and 50 degrees (40 degrees is the most aggressive; 50 degrees gives you the most control).

Now, place the control leg in the V-pocket, as shown in *Photo 2*. Start grinding one wing, then pull the tool away from the wheel and grind the other wing. Finally, blend the wings with the nose.

In the turning classes I teach in Provo, I recommend a 50-degree angle as the best starting point for tool control, as shown in *Photo 3*. If you get confused about sharpening angles, think of 90 degrees as no sharpened angle and a really steep angle as 30 degrees. A metal protractor like the General model shown in the photo is quite affordable. It's a good investment.

## Common mistakes

- **Not setting up the jig the same way each time.** The quicker you learn to produce a consistent grind, the faster you'll advance your skills. This method will get you back to the lathe quickly.
- **Over-grinding the nose of the tool.** Most new turners start grinding at the nose of the tool, then grind one wing, hit the nose again, grind the other wing, and finally return to the nose. This means you spend too much time on the nose and end up changing the profile. Don't do that! Follow the step-by-step instructions above.
- **Grinding in one sweep.** When you do this, you have a tendency to hesitate as you transition from the wing to the nose and from the nose to the wing. This causes a bird-beak grind, which is challenging to control.
- **Failure to keep the tool moving.** You will create flat or straight spots if you over-grind in one area.
- **Gripping the tool handle.** For better control, grip the tool at the grinding jig when you sharpen, as shown in *Photo 2*.

*Kirk DeHeer (kdeheer@cs.com) lives in Provo, Utah. He is a full-time woodturner and demonstrator.*

The Gouge Setup Jig will help you set the V-pocket at the proper distance from the grinding wheel for consistent bevels.

For best control of sharpening, hold the Vari-Grind in your hand. Avoid attempting to control by gripping the tool handle.

An inexpensive metal protractor will help you measure your tool bevels.

# Turners Test Sharpening Jigs

*AAW Members*

Most turners know the value of sharp tools, but few enjoy sharpening more than they like lathe work. For most it's a necessary chore. Many turners, as Clay Foster writes here, still prefer working freehand. But there is now an amazing variety of sharpening jigs on the market, and more and more turners are using them. Many turning teachers rely on jigs to help beginners get over the sharpening blues.

Because there are so many sharpening jigs on the market, the AW Journal asked members to discuss the ones they liked best.

## Sorby Fingernail Grinding Jig

When I attended a Robert Sorby demonstration at the Woodcraft store in Seattle, I was impressed with the fingernail grind on their new tools and ordered one of their Fingernail Grinding Jigs. When it arrived, I mounted it on the left wheel of my grinder (I have a Veritas jig mounted on the right hand wheel). I carefully set it up to the dimensions given on the instruction sheet that came with the jig and started to grind one of my 3/8-in. spindle gouges. I immediately had problems getting the long sweep back that I wanted.

Roger, my woodturning friend down the road who had attended the Sorby demonstration with me and also purchased one of the jigs, wasn't having any problems with his. A visit to Roger's shop, immediately showed why. I had a 3/4-in.-wide wheel, Roger had a 1-1/2 in. wide wheel. So, I called in an order and in a few days had a new 1-1/2 in. wheel on my grinder. That wider wheel made all of the difference in the world. The jig worked just the way I thought it should.

The gouge must stick out of the tool holder approximately two inches for the jig to work properly. It is pretty hard to measure this while holding the tool holder, trying to secure the tool in place in the holder, and at the same time tightening an Allen screw. I made a mark on my workbench two inches in from the edge. Now, I slip the gouge into the tool holder, press the tool holder against the edge of the bench, push the gouge through until it lines up with the mark on the bench, and tighten the set screw. Then I screw the little wheel down to check that the tool is properly oriented in the tool holder. The wheel should touch both edges of the flute.

The jig comes from the factory set to replicate the medium fingernail grind that Sorby puts on their fingernail-grind gouges. The angle of the grind looks to be about

Robert Sorby Fingernail Grinding Jig

65 degrees. With this angle of grind, my spindle gouge required a slightly different hold than I had been using on it. It was a bit too steep for good spindle work, but boy did it work great for bowls. You could start at the rim and cut in one continuous sweep to the center without a problem, just like the professionals. The factory setting worked great for my bowl gouges, but I finally modified the angle for my spindle gouges, they seem to work better with a longer angle.

I've been hand-grinding a fingernail grind on my bowl and spindle gouges for several years,

AW 13:4, p23, AW 14:1, p35

but each sharpening left me with a slightly different grind that required me to adjust my cutting angle. The Sorby jig eliminates this problem. The grind is repeatable and smooth from side to side, one continuous grind, no facets.
—*Fred Holder, Camano Island, WA*

## OneWay Wolverine System

OneWay Wolverine System

I was introduced to the Wolverine grinding system by Nick Cook while I was visiting the Georgia Association of Woodturners. Prior to that I had always sharpened by hand.

At present, I use the OneWay system in conjunction with sharpening by hand and I really like to use the system with students for the same reason Nick does. At a workshop, I don't have to spend all my time at the grinding wheel and can spend more time with my students.

As Nick showed me, the system is based on two mounts that attach permanently to the base under your grinder. Once the system is set up, it's simple to install two separate tool supports.

The first support or tool rest is a large flat adjustable platform fitted with a locking lever, making it easy to adjust. The large (3-in. X 5-in.) flat surface is ideal for scrapers and parting tools. The second support is a sliding V-block fixture, which supports the base of your tool, allowing you to maintain a consistent bevel as the tool is rolled against the wheel of the grinder. It's good for roughing gouges and deep-fluted bowl gouges.

The optional Vari-Grind jig, made to fit the sliding V-block fixture, enables you to create a fingernail grind on spindle gouges or the side-grind on deep-fluted bowl gouges.

Personally, I would purchase the Wolverine Grinding System because of one other attachment, the dressing attachment. I've used everything from the star wheel dresser to dressing sticks and I like the Wolverine dressing attachment best by far. Now, I true and clean my wheels two or three times a day rather than waiting until they are totally loaded up and ineffective.

The attachment consists of a support arm, a holder for the diamond tip and the diamond tip that does the dressing. The support arm slides into the grinding jig base and dressing is accomplished by sliding the diamond-tip holder back and forth across the support arm. Fine adjustments are accomplished via a knob on the diamond-tip holder. I found it useful to apply a bit of wax on the support arm to allow the holder to move more freely.

The only attachment that I do not use is the skew grinding attachment. It works fine, but I prefer a more radical angle on my skews. I also grind a radius that I am not able to obtain with a jig.

The Vari-Grind attachment will allow you to obtain both a fingernail grind as well as a side grind. It works beautifully. However, you might consider grinding the base of the support to allow it to pivot in the V-arm a little better. This just allows for a little smoother operation.

The gouge is held in place in the Vari-Grind jig via a screw-and-leaf-spring clamp that puts pressure on the flute of the tool and keeps it from rotating while sharpening. After numerous grindings you will probably run out of flute and the leaf spring will no longer seat on the flute. Not to worry. You can eyeball the position of the gouge, lock it in position and extend the life of the tool.

Probably the biggest disadvantage of the Wolverine system is that if you are organizationally challenged as I am, you end up with a lot of accessories laying around the shop getting in your way. The solution is really very simple: hang them up. A few spare minutes, a bit of pegboard, and the disaster area becomes manageable.

I would caution that the Wolverine Grinding System or any grinding system is not a panacea for all your sharpening problems. Ultimately, you still need to know what you want that tool to look like and what you want it to do after you have finished grinding it. A jig will help, but it will not do it all.
—*Bob Rosand, Bloomsburg, PA, with Nick Cook, Atlanta, GA*

## Wolverine Tips

Prior to owning a sharpening jig, I struggled to get acceptable edges on my tools, especially the gouges, and fell into the bad habit of delaying sharpening at the expense of good quality turning.

Happily my Wolverine jig has given me a new outlook on woodturning. My tools now have uniform, facet-free grinds, and I spend more quality time at the lathe and less time fussing and cussing at the grinding wheel.

I believe that grinding jigs can provide smooth, reproducible grinds in the hands of the less experienced and less talented woodturner. With a bit of practice and careful adherence to the manufacturer's instructions, it is not too difficult to get satisfactory grinds. These jigs, however, will not do your thinking for you. As Bob Rosand notes in his commentary on the Wolverine system, "You still need to know what you want your tool to look like and what you want it to do after you have finished grinding."

There are an infinite number of settings (and resulting grinds) available from a gouge grinding jig, such as the Vari-Grind attachment of the Wolverine jig. So, unless you've got the Sorby fingernail gouge, it takes a little study and practice with the attachment to get in the ball park and ultimately to get the desired grind on your tool. Once you have established your grind, subsequent re-sharpenings are duck soup.

For those of you who own or contemplate buying the Wolverine system, I'd like to pass on a few tips on getting reproducible grinds with the jig. To begin with, prior to sharpening, I coat the bevel of my tool with a waterproof, felt-tip red marking pen and periodically inspect it during grinding. When all of the red has disappeared, I know that I've worked over the entire bevel from one side to the other and from heel to tip. I, of course, also watch for sparks over the top of the tool, to avoid burning the steel.

A second tip is to keep written records of the jig settings for each individual tool. Being a retired engineer, I keep prodigious records of my turning activities, so the first time I sharpen each tool to the desired grind, I log the following data in my notebook:

1. The horizontal distance (in mms.) that the V-arm juts out from the end of the clamping fixture. I measure from the front end (the end nearest you) of the clamping fixture to the front end of the V notch tool handle support. This is all you have to record for roughing gouges, parting tools and skew chisels.

2. In addition to the V-arm measurement above, when using the Vari-Grind attachment (for spindle and bowl gouges), I measure the distance from the end of the tool tip to the front end (the side closest to the tool tip) of the U-shaped clamp; and,

3. I measure the setting of the angle arm adjacent to the wing nut on the Vari-Grind jig. To help you with this there are seven unnumbered graduated lines inscribed on the attachment by the manufacturer. I gave them numbers: 0.0, 0.5, 1.0, etc., up to 3.0. For a regular fingernail grind, with the fixture set in the "up" position, the reading is 0.0 or just beyond 0.0 (the arm on my Vari-Grind goes just a little beyond the zero line.) In the extreme "down" position (for a side grind), the reading is 3.0 or just beyond 3.0 (the arm of my Vari-Grind goes just a little beyond the last mark.) A mid-arm location would be 1.5. Currently, I've been using this position for my gouges to get a medium fingernail grind. Something a little further down would be 1.9, etc.

With the above information in hand, whenever you need to re-sharpen a tool, you just flip open your notebook and set the V-arm distance and the Vari-Grind tool position and grind angle number and you get a grind identical to the previous one.

Before you start the grinder, it is always a good idea to eyeball the tool from the side to be sure the bevel is on the wheel. If not, make a minor adjustment, usually on the V-arm setting. As your tools shorten with many repeated sharpenings, and your grinding wheel shrinks in diameter, your settings will change a bit, so update your notebook as time goes on. I find the above practice to be much better than marking the tool shanks, the V-arm shaft and the Vari-Grind attachment with a marking pen because you get as many pen marks as you have tools and the marks wear off and you soon get confused. Instead, record your settings in your notebook.

*—Frank Koubek, Cincinnati, OH*

## Glaser Jig

Having taken enough turning courses to be able to grind the fingernail gouge freehand, I was always haunted by the fact that no matter how hard I try I could never grind a gouge without facets. Since I felt this was a shortcoming in my technique I began to use a jig. This experience came in handy, when, working for a turning supplies dealer, I was assigned to grind the tools before they were sent to customers. Since the company was using the Glaser jig I taught myself how to use it. Use it we did. We ground hundreds of gouges: short, medium and long grinds with swept edges, radical grinds with various swept edges, all without one, single facet. So it was natural for me to use the same jig in my shop.

The Glaser jig is an articulated arm with a pivot point in the floor. The jig is beautifully made to Glaser's exacting specifications using hard maple. The tool is held in a V-block guide 3" from the edge on the wood block.

The jig is somewhat fussy to set up as there are a number of measurements to be made and calculations needed to locate the pivot point on just the right spot

Glaser Jig

on the floor. Fortunately, the directions provided are clear and simple. Following these instructions carefully will insure a correct set up the first try.

The purpose of the jig is to provide a simple and repeatable method to grind fingernail shapes on spindle and bowl gouges. The articulated arm is to provide different bevel angles at the nose of the gouge as compared to the side of the tool. It also has two suggested settings: one for spindle gouges (26 degrees) and the other (37 degrees) for bowl gouges.

After set up, using the jig could not be simpler. Just clamp the tool into the articulated head as directed, choose the angle setting for spindle or bowl gouge, and sharpen it. As the instructions explain, the easiest method is to grind the profile of the finished fingernail shape before clamping it in the jig, then use the jig to sharpen to that edge. Using 8-in. diameter white wheels (80 grit and 120 grit) running at 3600 rpm, it is, at first, somewhat unsettling to present the tool without a standard tool rest. However, with a smooth running grinder that has trued and balanced wheels, there is little bouncing on the stone. The fingernail shape comes freely off the wheel with simple hand motions. No compound movements to ride the stone are necessary to achieve the fingernail shape.

I use the jig to sharpen all my spindle gouges and all my bowl gouges including the big 3/4-in. gouge. The jig is capable of sharpening any style of cutting edge from the most benign flat grind to the most radical swept back grind. The jig does them all and is easily re-settable so that a new edge removes as little steel as possible. The best thing is that I no longer feel any guilt about having a faceted tool but also in the knowledge that I cannot blame a poor grind on a tool for bad turning.
*—Angelo Iafrate, New Canaan, CT*

## Ellsworth Jig

The Ellsworth jig does what it is designed to do and that is, put David's swept-back grind on the 5/8-in. Superflute gouge, also known as the Ellsworth Signature Gouge. I learned about the tool when I attended David's class; I learned to use the tool standing at my lathe. In class, David taught us how to grind the tool by hand, no jig. The jig wasn't invented that time. I learned to sharpen the gouge pretty well in my shop, though the grind never was exactly as he taught us and I always had lots of facets on my bevel. Then, David came up with a wooden jig. It made a genuine improvement in the facets removal. I did not take the time to precisely setup the jig stand so I never quite achieved a replication of his grind, but it was close and acceptable, at least to me. Then, recently he sent me a new cast-aluminum version. It came with detailed instructions on how to set everything up, so I did. Bingo! I can now sharpen the thing the same way every time in less than 10 seconds. That's a good thing.

However, the Ellsworth jig is not intended for, nor can it be used for, any other tool. It is a single-purpose jig, for the 5/8-in. superflute Ellsworth gouge.

The jig doesn't make me a better turner. It doesn't improve my designs. It just allows me to grind the tool the same way every time. Any person who wants to be able to do the same thing would benefit from having this jig. This would

Ellsworth Jig

have to be primarily David's past students, who spent a couple of hours of a Friday morning in David's shop agonizing over the correct way to sharpen that tool.

If you can't attend David's weekend class, but want to learn his gouge techniques, his sharpening video is a must. It is not a glitzy, MTV-style tape, but you're going to learn far more than you expect. It is an Ellsworth style presentation (read: nothing fancy.) It is a down-and-dirty instructional. The shots are clear and steady. He has the turner in mind. You want to see when somebody shows you how to do something. The camera angles let you see... up close and personal. The video quality is excellent.

After demonstrating each type of cut using his signature gouge -- roughing cuts, hogging cuts, smoothing cuts, shear cutting and back cutting -- he shows sharpening techniques using the new sharpening jig. I can't disagree with what Clay Foster writes here about knowing how to sharpen your tools freehand without jigs. He's correct, of course. But, on the other side, when I am in the throes of turning and the rhythm is flowing, I don't want it interrupted by an inept experience at the grinder. And, I like the fact that I can get the same tip and edge every time. That way, the tool action becomes predictable. (At least I can't fault the tool when I mess up!)

This tape does not address issues of design, but it does show the techniques we can use for fixing that questionable curve. He shows how to avoid the annoying little nub in the bottom of our bowls. There is essential information about how to get a clean cut on a natural-edge bowl. I think that's pretty neat. Especially when all the cuts utilize only one tool.

*—Dick Tuttle, Schwenksville, PA*

## Tormek Sharpening System

The Tormek water-cooled sharpening system is made in Sweden and is one of the most versatile sharpening systems on the market.

The Tormek can be customized for cabinetmakers, woodturners, and wood carvers by selecting from the company's wide variety of jigs and guides for the particular blades or tools that you need to grind.

If you have to sharpen a lot of different cutting edges in your shop, everything from carving gouges to scissors, the Tormek variety of guides and attachments might be just the thing for you. All of these accessories are designed specifically to go on the company's grinders. These grinders can run both water-cooled grinding wheels, which are available in different grits, and a leather honing wheel.

For the woodturner, gouges (both bowl and spindle) are easily sharpened and maintained with the SVD 180 jig shown here, which can be easily adjusted to a particular grind that meets the desires of the individual turner. The SVS 50 multi-grinding jig makes sharpening the skew chisel easy and has proven to be very useful in my shop.

The Tormek sharpening system can prolong the usefulness of gouges by sharpening without grinding away so much metal. I find that the skew is easier to sharpen on the Tormek than on a conventional grinder. The addition of the profiled honing wheel is helpful for polishing the flute of gouges and the ground surface of all tools. The profiled honing wheel is actually a rotating profiled leather strop.

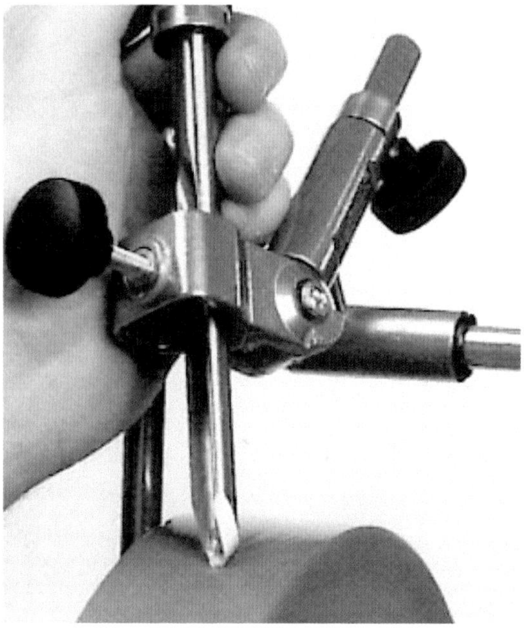

Tormek Universal Gouge Jig

Although I do not use the Tormek exclusively, I have been using it more and more and find it a useful addition to my shop.

*—Willard Baxter, Gainsville GA*

## In praise of jiglessness

In the beginning, there were no jigs for grinding a deep fluted bowl gouge with a long cutting edge. My first attempts at freehand grinding produced a bevel that looked like a plowed field. It had more facets than Liz Taylor's diamond collection. After a little practice and a few inches of gouge, I eventually got the hang of it. Grinding is now a reflexive action that takes very little time to produce a sharp tool with the exact profile I want. For the person desiring to grow beyond occasional turning, I think free hand grinding is the best option.

All of the sharpening jigs I have seen will do a good job of grinding a gouge, some with more alacrity than others, but none of them are as fast and convenient as freehand. Like most people, if something is quick and convenient, I am likely to do it more often. Obviously, this includes tool sharpening. I've never met anyone that I thought sharpened their gouge too often, but I've known a lot of turners who put it off until it was too late and made a mess at the lathe.

Learning to grind a gouge freehand develops graceful movements and a light touch of the hand. Can you think of another related activity where these skills would be desirable? Hint: if you don't know the correct answer to this question, it may explain why your work has that awkward, bludgeoned quality to it.

Freehand grinding is an acquired skill, just like any other aspect of woodturning. You learn it by doing it over and over again. In order to consume less tool while learning to grind, try practicing with the grinder turned off. You can feel the bevel matching up to the wheel and the correct arc of the tool through space without watching your expensive gouge being transported to the shop floor in a meteoric shower of sparks.

In the end, it comes down to what you choose to spend: your time or your money. You can spend your time developing a skill, or your money on a jig that will almost do it for you. Either choice is valid, and no proponent of either method has any right to feel superior. I have no regrets that I had to learn how to grind a gouge the old fashioned way when there was no choice. It's still the choice I would make now.

*—Clay Foster, Krum, FX*

## Sharpening Carbide Cutters

I figured out a way to sharpen Easy Finisher carbide cutters. I like using carbide cutters, but they are $18 and eventually need to be sharpened (or thrown out). Sharpening is easy. The cutters pictured are the Easy Rough Rider and Easy Finisher tools, but almost any round or square cutter should work in this simple jig.

Mount a small length of hardwood into a 4-jaw chuck and turn the end round. Next, find a wood screw that fits the hole in the carbide cutter and fills the recess area for the screw and is positioned below the surface on the cutter. I used a number x 1" (25 mm) screw in the setup shown. However, carbide tool manufacturers would recommend obtaining the same tapered-head screw that mounts the cutter in its handle.

Insert a small drill bit into a Jacobs chuck in the tailstock and bore a small pilot hole in the center of the turning. The screw should screw in snugly but not split the wood. If the hole is not centered or the screw is not tight, the cutter could move around and be sharpened unevenly. Do not over-tighten the screw.

Tighten the carbide cutter up to the wood handle and if necessary, turn away more excess wood for good access. Spin the cutter to a moderate RPM. Use a flat diamond file and hold it against the proper angle of the carbide cutter. You may have to experiment a little, but the spinning cutter will get a razor-sharp edge with a little patience.

If the cutter is flat on top, it is most important to dress the top surface. The diameter of the cutter will slowly decrease with repeated sharpening, but you will get a lot more use out of these cutters first.

This procedure does generate fine carbide dust, which can be bad news for your lungs. Consequently, wear a dust respirator whenever you sharpen carbide, and if you find yourself doing it a lot, figure out a way to add a water mist to the setup.

*—Ken Rizza, Mike Hunter and Phil Vetra*

# Safety Lessons: Sharpening Jigs

*Jim Rodgers*

As the use of sharpening jigs increases, so, too, do the instances of sharpening accidents. Injuries that result from fragmented grinding wheels and tools and holders that have slipped have sent woodturners to the hospital with serious injuries to hands and/or eyes.

Sharpening jigs were developed so that we could quickly and repeatedly produce a tool shape, bevel, and edge. When using these jigs, however, woodworkers need to be aware of some potential dangers. Tools can slide off the face of the grinding wheels and wedge between the wheel and the frame of the grinder; the arms of sharpening jigs can slip outward away from the wheel, causing the tip of the tool to move down the surface of the grinding wheel until the tool grabs at the wheel's equator and instantly wedges itself, fracturing the wheel and potentially injuring the operator's hand; tools can slip forward in the tool holder itself causing similar problems.

While mechanical failure of sharpening jigs contributes to some injuries, human error is usually the cause. Here's why:

- The person sharpening the tool is distracted and the tool no longer rides on the wheel. A quick turn of a person's head can easily cause the movement of a tool off a 1"-wide grinding wheel, jamming it between the wheel and the body of the grinder.
- An improper handhold on the jig can cause fingers to be driven into the still-running grinding wheel.
- Too much pressure is applied to the tool causing mechanical slippage of the jig's arm.
- Improper grinding-jig geometry is set, placing the tip of the tool too close to the maximum diameter of the wheel (the equator).
- The process of sharpening tools is hurried.
- Small-diameter tools are improperly placed in jigs not meant to handle their smaller size.

## Proper use of grinding jigs

- Firmly lock the jig's extension arm and recheck it by pushing or pulling on it.
- Establish a more acute bevel angle on your turning tool. Placing the tool high on the sharpening wheel's surface reduces the possibility of an accident.
- Reduce the amount of downward pressure applied during sharpening; this will save tool steel and reduce heat buildup.

Using a simple shopmade template to set up your sharpening jig for repeatable distances saves time and tool wear.

Wrong way! If the sharpening jig slips, fingers will contact the rotating wheel before the jig does.

AW 24:4, p25

A safer way to hold the jig is on the top. If a slip occurs, the hand is protected.

Potential danger: Using a long fixture arm and a blunt sharpening angle brings the tip of the tool too close to the wheel's equator. If the arm of the jig slips or too much pressure is exerted, it could cause the tool to jam against the wheel.

## Wear safety gear

A faceshield or safety glasses should be worn while at the sharpening station. Eye injury is possible while sharpening as a result of flying debris. When dressing a wheel for cleaning or reshaping, wear a dust mask. The aluminum oxide dust from a grinding wheel is potentially damaging to lungs.

## Proper hold

When holding the sharpening jig, never place your hand between the jig and the grinding wheel. Place one hand on the handle of the tool and the other on top of the jig. Accidents occur when the hand hits the rotating wheel during a slippage.

## Light touch

Sharpening should be done with a light touch; this reduces the amount of metal being removed and the heat buildup during the sharpening. A light touch also allows the operator to react quickly when a slippage occurs, perhaps saving a finger.

## New sharpening jigs

Until recently, most sharpening jigs managed the sharpening geometry well, but still allowed for uncontrolled side movements that contributed to most accidents. Currently two manufactures, Sharp Fast and Oneway, have introduced jigs that eliminate the accidental sideways movement while maintaining the proper sharpening geometry. As a teacher of woodturning at both high school and adult levels, I would not be without such a jig!

---

*Jim Rodgers is past president of the Bay Area Woodturners and director of the turning programs for Mt. Diablo Unified School District. He can be contacted at jlrodgers@aol.com or jlrodgers.com.*

Better: Create a more acute bevel angle on your tool, which will place it higher up on the wheel in a safer position when sharpening.

Consider learning how to hand sharpen turning tools. This allows you to place a toolrest close to the grinding wheel, eliminating many potential dangers.

# Virtues of Wet Grinding

*Terry Martin*

More than 30 years ago, an old-school turner showed me how to sharpen my tools freehand on a grinder, and I practiced for years to get it right. I burnt tool edges, ground multi-faceted bevels, and wasted a lot of valuable metal. I considered these efforts a rite of passage and mastered the process reasonably well. I was convinced it was the best way and never saw the need to change.

On a good day, I was able to get an edge that would produce crisp shavings that flew off the tool in long ribbons. When asked, "What angle do you grind your tool bevels?" I would joke, "What day is it?" With the development of jigs for sharpening, I was approached by manufacturers and offered a chance to try their equipment. My response was always, "No, I'm fine, thanks. I can do what I want quickly and easily, and I don't need a jig to do it." In reality, although what I did was sufficient, it was not as good as it could be.

## Change of thinking

A set of unusual circumstances combined to change my mind. I traveled to Ireland to demonstrate at Glenn Lucas's woodturning school, where he and I discussed the comparative merits of different grinds. He showed me how his grind does exactly what he wants every time. He then told me something that really affected me: "I get return students all the time, but they don't come back to learn to turn. They come back to learn to sharpen. It's far and away the most difficult thing a beginner has to master. That's why I always teach them to use a jig, so they can concentrate on doing what they want to do—turn wood." Glenn showed me how effectively he uses his wet grinder, and although I did my demonstrations with my regular grind, the seed had been planted.

It might have ended there, but back in Australia, I was watching Theo Haralampou demonstrate turning to a large crowd at a tradeshow. The main thing he was asked was how he got his tools so sharp. When he explained he always uses a wet grinder and showed them how he does it, they were deeply impressed. When Theo asked me if I wanted to try a wet grinder, I declined. My reaction was just the kind of habitual response that came from set-in-my-ways thinking.

Sharpening a bowl gouge

Theo insisted and invited me to his shop. A week later, he showed me how to grind and hone my bowl gouge, and I learned I had been wrong. He reproduced my preferred grind exactly using the wet-grinder's jig. We mounted a piece of wood onto the lathe, practiced a few cuts, and I could not believe how easy it was. After just a few passes, I turned to Theo and said, "I feel like I'm cutting twice as well!"

I now have my own wet grinder, a Tormek, and I was able to master the sharpening process quickly because of the excellent handbook and demonstration DVD that comes with it. Also, there are helpful tutorials online covering every aspect of wet sharpening. Even

AW 29:3, p22

The wheel rotates away from the tool's cutting edge.

The leather honing wheel removes the grooves from the wet wheel.

How sweet it is!

The edge of a gouge sharpened on my dry grinder

The same edge after wet sharpening and honing

better, I found objective evidence to support my impressions that wet grinding is superior in an article by Robbie Farrance, addressing all of the questions on comparative quality of edge, durability, and quality of cut. His conclusions are backed by microscopic analysis and timed cutting tests with the results shown in graph form. It is a thorough investigation and technically minded readers will appreciate his commitment to unbiased analysis: (tormek.com/en/leaflet/pdf/wet_or_dry_en.pdf)

Farrance's conclusions can be summarized:

- After initial shaping, wet grinding is simple, quick, accurate, and repeatable.
- Wet grinding creates a polished, burr-free edge, does not overheat the tool, causes less friction in use, and so extends the life of the edge.
- Tool life is prolonged because less material is removed.
- Wet-ground tools produce cleaner cuts with more than double the turning time between sharpening.
- In one test, after 18 minutes of continuous turning, the wet-ground tool was cutting 3.5 times faster than the dry-ground tool.

I agree with Farrance's conclusions. The more I have learned about wet grinding, the more enthusiastic I become. Dry grinding is likely to affect the temper of your tools and even if you don't burn the edge, the heat has an effect on the integrity of the metal. After wet grinding, you are cutting with metal that has not been substantially altered from its tempered state. This means the tools stay sharp longer, so you don't have to sharpen as often. Some people have never experienced using a truly sharp tool, but when they do, they will find it takes less force to cut and it cuts so cleanly that the savings in abrasives alone are significant.

Additional benefits in safety are worth considering. There is none of the hot and dangerous debris that flies off a dry grinder. Slow-speed wet grinders never disintegrate, so there is no need to wear a faceshield. Theo made a good point about the relative safety of the two systems: "If you accidentally touch a spinning wet wheel, nothing happens, but if you touch a dry wheel...."

The only drawback of wet grinding is that initial shaping is very slow. My Tormek's black wheel is relatively coarse and makes the process quicker, but there is a place for pre-grinding to speed up the process of reshaping a tool. To facilitate using a dry grinder before wet sharpening, Tormek produces a bench-grinder mounting set that will give you exactly the same shape you can then take to your wet grinder for finishing. This jig works well. For grinding to reshape a bevel, I would use a ceramic wheel, or one of the more recent CBN wheels.

There are other wet grinders on the market—Grizzly, Delta, Makita, Work Sharp, JET, Northern Industrial—and they will also do a good job. I am certain any of them will produce a better result than dry grinding. Because Tormek regularly improves its system, that's the brand I selected. Try wet sharpening; like me, you will be amazed how much better your turning experience is.

*Terry Martin is a wood artist, writer, and curator who lives and works in Brisbane, Australia. He can be contacted at eltel@optusnet.com.au.*

# Narrow-Belt Sharpening

*Kenneth A. Ray*

I have been using a 1-in. X 42-in. belt grinder to sharpen my lathe tools. I still use a 6-in. bench grinder on certain tools, but the belt grinder, with its flat, adjustable table, offers significant advantages:

- The tools are laid flat on the table and never lifted during any of the grinding operations. This greatly simplifies the sharpening of side-ground gouges.
- By using a set of simple plywood templates, the table can be quickly set to different angles. Thus the face of each tool can be presented at the exact appropriate angle so that a very small amount of metal is removed. Setting the table angle to a 6inch-diameter round wheel is rather difficult.
- The belt can be quickly changed, often without moving the table, from coarse for fast shaping to medium for a finished edge.
- The long belt seems to dissipate heat better than a small-diameter wheel, so that tool edges are less prone to overheating.

In spite of these advantages, the belt methods do not supplant a regular grinder when a concave bevel is preferable, as for beading and parting tools. Some prefer a hollow grind on skews also. *(Photo 1)*

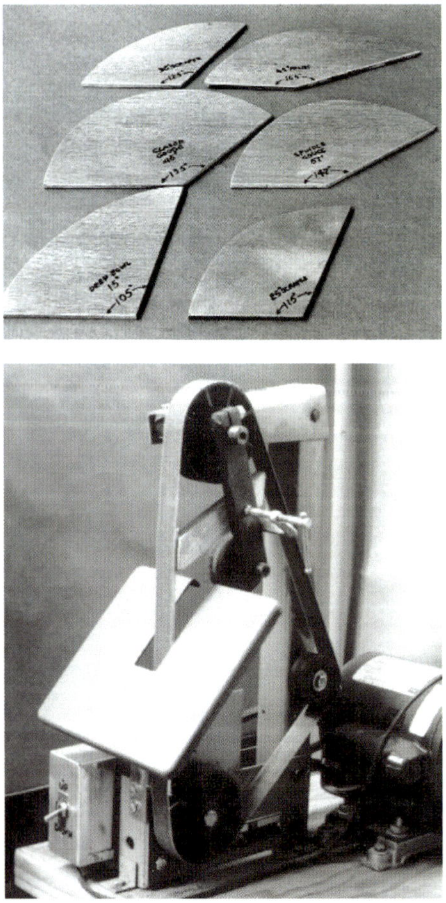

1. Author's 1-in. belt grinder and angle templates for flat-grind tool sharpening.

The grinder I use is a Delta. Any 1-in. or 2-in. belt grinder can be used, provided the table has the ability to tilt down about 60 degrees from the horizontal. If the table as supplied cannot do that or moves too far from the belt when tilted to the extreme, an auxiliary table can be added. The table of the Delta grinder can be moved closer to the belt as needed.

I tighten the table pivot bolt so that firm pressure is required to tilt the table; a jam nut maintains the position. The table angles are set with plywood templates, as shown in the photos. The template angle is the sharpening angle (measured from the vertical) plus 90 degrees. The Delta grinder has a rather large table, which is convenient for long and heavy tools. On small and miniature tools the tool handle will interfere with flat positioning on the table. Place a small piece of wood of the required thickness under the shaft of the tool to provide clearance during sharpening.

I have added a motor-reversing switch to run the belt backwards when sharpening scrapers. It is not necessary to reorient the belt, even if it is lap-spliced. Running the belt upward past the tool produces a more pronounced burr, essential for good scraper performance.

I use a 1/2 horsepower (1/4-horsepower would be adequate), 3450rpm motor and a pulley ratio that results in a belt speed of 3,951 feet per minute. I have not felt the need to experiment with other speeds.

For general sharpening, I use a 120-grit aluminum oxide closed-coat belt, the least expensive version available. I have tried many different belts, ranging from medium to premium grade, and I find the extra cost is not justified. A butt splice will give a much smoother performance than a lap splice. I have never had a belt fail at the splice. If a large amount of metal needs to be removed for the initial shaping, I recommend a blue zirconium 80-grit belt.

You can achieve a finer surface with a 220-grit (or finer) belt, at the expense of a slower grind and possible overheating. You can obtain a highly polished finish by using a leather belt charged with a polishing compound and run backwards, away from the cutting edge. The left hand supports the tool close to the edge, and any onset of overheating can be detected before the metal loses temper. Dipping the tool in a large container of cool water will help keep the temperature down. I use a brace against the back of the belt platen to prevent angle changes, however slight, when pressing the

AW 9:4, p24

2. To sharpen a side-ground gouge, the tool is kept flat on the table and the handle is swung from side to side as the tool is rolled. The more swing and roll, the more pronounced the side-grind.

tool against the belt. The pressure required is very light, making it easy to maintain smooth movements during sharpening.

You sharpen a straight-ended scraper simply by laying it flat on the table and sliding it from side to side. I am in the habit of moving even narrow tools across the face of the belt. This helps in keeping the tool cool and in evening the wear on the belt. I sharpen a round-nose scraper using the first finger of the left hand as a pivot and swinging the handle from side to side. A quick glance at the result after the first momentary contact will show a shiny line across the entire bevel, confirming that the angle has been duplicated exactly.

I use two angles for scrapers. The majority are sharpened at 35 degrees (all bevel angles are measured from the vertical, the tool horizontal). Some small narrow scrapers I sharpen at 25 degrees, since the larger angle would remove too much material from the underside of the tool. Steep-angled chisels, such as Rude Osolnik's round-point chisels, are ground at a 57-degree angle, using the 147-degree template. I chamfer the underside edges of all flat tools such as scrapers and skews to slide better across the tool rest.

Spindle gouges and large roughing gouges are also ground at 57 degrees using the 147-degree template and keeping the tool flat on the table, except, instead of sliding or swinging the tool, you roll it. Small-diameter spindle gouges are held at right angles to the belt and simply rolled back and forth along the table. A large-diameter roughing gouge may require a change of position on the table to keep it in range of the belt. This will not show up in the finished surface. A flat diamond paddle is useful for touching up edges between grindings, and a tapered diamond rod is indispensible for removing the light burr inside gouges and polishing the flute.

To create the side-grind on a deep bowl gouge you again keep the tool flat on the table and now do two movements at once: swing the handle from side to side, rolling the tool slightly as you swing. Start the roll when the tool passes center and increase it progressively until reaching maximum roll at the end of the swing, as shown in the photos.

There is nothing sacred about the amount of swing and roll; it can vary from a mild side grind shown on the Jerry Glaser gouge to a more pronounced grind on a Sorby deep bowl gouge. The relief angles shown in the photo are arbitrary. For the sake of convenience, I use the 147-degree template on the Glaser gouge to get a 57-degree relief angle and the 135-degree template to get a 45-degree relief on the Sorby gouge. I grind the new 7/i6-in. M4 detail gouge by Glaser at a 57-degree sharpening angle and use a 155-degree template to get a 65-degree relief angle. If you are using different angles on your tools, make your templates to correspond.

There are many variations possible using the belt and table system. The photos show my version of the nib-gouge grind by Melvyn Firmager. I use the 147-degree template and rock the tool slightly on either side of center before completing the roll as you would for a normal gouge. This creates an S-curved edge on each side with a nib in the center and two pronounced wings at the top. These raised wings will cut quickly and smoothly but are prone to catching in some situations.

3. Three different grinds: A mild side grind on a Glaser gouge, left. Center, a more pronounced side grind on a Sorby deep bowl gouge. And right, a nib-gouge grind.

# Shop-Built Sharpening Jigs

*King Heiple*

As fingernail grinds for turning tools became steadily more popular, I struggled to learn to create them freehand. And with persistence I gradually acquired reasonable proficiency, but I never could produce exactly the same angle each time and often had less than perfect results.

After buying two different commercial systems for fingernail grinds, I got much better results. But many of my fellow turners in the Northcoast Woodturners chapter in Cleveland were reluctant to make such an investment for something they doubted could make a difference in their work. When our club decided to purchase its own grinder to go with its three lathes, though, I suddenly decided that the club had to have a dedicated sharpening jig system to be really useful. In light of the club's budget, I decided to build one from scratch.

The result of my work is shown in this article. I used it at home for a month and now prefer my gouge-holding jig over the commercial ones I also own.

Author uses his sharpening system to grind a large roughing-out gouge. The support arm can be adjusted to accommodate all sizes of gouges, so that each can be ground to the correct angle every time. The rest at right can be used for scrapers and skews, or can be replaced with a second gouge support.

## Base and slides

The only metal parts are two 5/16-in. T-nuts and matching thumbscrews, available from any local hardware, and enough construction screws to assemble. Glue all the joints together during assembly as well; the unit has to withstand lots of vibration over time. Make the base first, as shown in Figure 1, then custom fit the slides to move easily. It's a good idea to make two slides at once, to avoid the hassle of changing the slide between the two wheels. By having an economical way to obtain two slides, you're already better off than you would be with a commercial unit.

Figure 1 represents the side view of the grinder on its base. The height of the wood block will vary, depending upon whether your grinder has 8-in., 7-in. or 6-in. diameter wheels. Size the pieces so that the pivot dimple in the block is 4 in. below the midpoint of the face of your wheel. When I'm sharpening/grinding a bowl gouge the distance from the face of the wheel will be about 7 in. Vary this to set the nose angle on your bowl gouge. I set mine to get 65 degrees but you may use a slightly different angle. This system will also do a spindle gouge very nicely, but the slide will be moved in towards the wheel until the nose angle is closer to 45-degrees. Again, you may prefer something slightly different.

I built this base from 3/4-in.-thick plywood, carpenter's glue, and screws. Note that you have to match fairly closely the centerline distance between your grinder wheels. In addition, after laying it out carefully, put in your T-nuts before assembly as it would be impossible after it is together. Better also if you recess the T-nuts flush to avoid catching your slide. Any 2x2-in. stock would make the slides, but I used some left over maple as it

AW 14:4, p28

will be more durable and dent less from the thumbscrew. The slides should move easily in their tunnels.

If you put the grinder at the front edge of your base you will have trouble using the thumbscrews. Keep its base 3 in. back from the front edge of your base.

## The gouge holding jig

The various components of Figure 3 detail the Gouge Holding jig. Note that the figure has a dimensional scale along its top edge, as the dimensions of this need to be accurate. If the scale lines are not 1 in. (dots = 1/4 in.) apart on the illustration, enlarge (or reduce) for a more accurate copy.

This jig requires one 5/16-in. T-nut and matching 1-1/2-in. thumbscrew, plus 6 in. of 5/16-in. metal rod (which could even be from an 8-in. carriage bolt). Use any fine-grained hard wood for this jig. Trim to 1/2-in. thickness. Note that the grain is run vertically on the sides, as it must resist tension in this direction. While you're at it, cut yourself enough pieces to make three or four jigs at once. You probably will spoil one or more and you may want to have an extra one besides.

Cut the strips for the bottom first, and drill for the pivot rod and T-nut. Put in the T-nut before assembly as it will be buried and impossible to reach later. Again, it should be flush with the wood surface. The angle for the pivot rod needs to be fairly close to 130-degrees from the horizontal (or 50-degrees measured the other way). If the angle is off significantly, ream out its hole a bit and use epoxy or thick super-glue to set the rod at the correct angle. The lower end of the pivot should be rounded and smooth and make sure the upper end does not protrude into the center opening.

The author's simple jig, used in conjunction with his shop-built support arm, makes it possible for anyone to obtain consistently perfect results when grinding the fingernail profile favored by many contemporary turners.

The side pieces (Figure 3B) need to be carefully shouldered until the center opening is just a bit (1/32 in.) wider than the widest gouge you will need to sharpen, for example 21/32 in. for a 5/8-in. gouge. And then you can cut the top strip to match this spacing.

A metal strip of any kind cemented into the top of the opening, as shown in Fig. 3B, will prevent your gouge edges from eroding your jig. When the unit has been completely assembled and aligned, and the glue is dry, trim it on a disk sander and taper the end as is shown in Fig. 3C, so that the corners of the jig do not hit the grindstone.

To make the jig usable with 1/2-in. diameter or smaller gouges, make a 30-degree V-shaped centering strip, as shown in Figs. 3B and 3D. It should fit loosely and move up easily to clamp in a smaller gouge. A small bent finishing nail at each end will prevent it from falling out.

Although this jig is primarily designed for bowl gouges, it does work quite well on spindle gouges. You may not wish to bring the grind back quite so far for spindle gouges.

Take one of the several jigs you made and increase the angle between the gouge and rod to 145 degrees (or 35 degrees measured the other way) to produce a shorter side bevel. My entire grinding system was finished with water-based polyurethane. It's a simple-to-apply, durable, and easy-to-clean finish.

## Scraper or freehand rest

For sharpening a scraper, cut-off tool or performing some other semi-freehand sharpening job, some sort of steady rest is very helpful. The one in in the drawing offers many possibilities. Go back and add a vertical 3/4-in. hole in each of your slides, 1-1/4 in. ahead of the V.

Cut a support block 1-1/2-in. X 2-1/4in. X 8-in. long and put a V on one edge to match the V on your slides. With it in place snugly in the V, mark the end through the hole in the slide for drilling (a dowel center is handy for this). Drill a vertical 3/4-in. hole in the end and glue in a 4-to-5-in. length of 3/4-in. turned dowel.

Now trim and sand the piece until it is a snug knock-in fit. Leave the dowel long enough to make it easy to knock out.

Pick the angle you like to grind scrapers at (mine are about 15 degrees) and mark the block to be trimmed for your rest platform so that its front edge is at the midpoint of the wheel.

The essentials of this rest are shown in the drawings. A similar one with just a round rod for a platform is also handy.

## Fingernail grind on a bowl gouge

If you are starting out with a conventional standard grind, the kind you might expect straight-from-the factory, as shown in Figure 4 (or even squarer), begin by putting a 65-degree nose angle on it as in

Figure 1

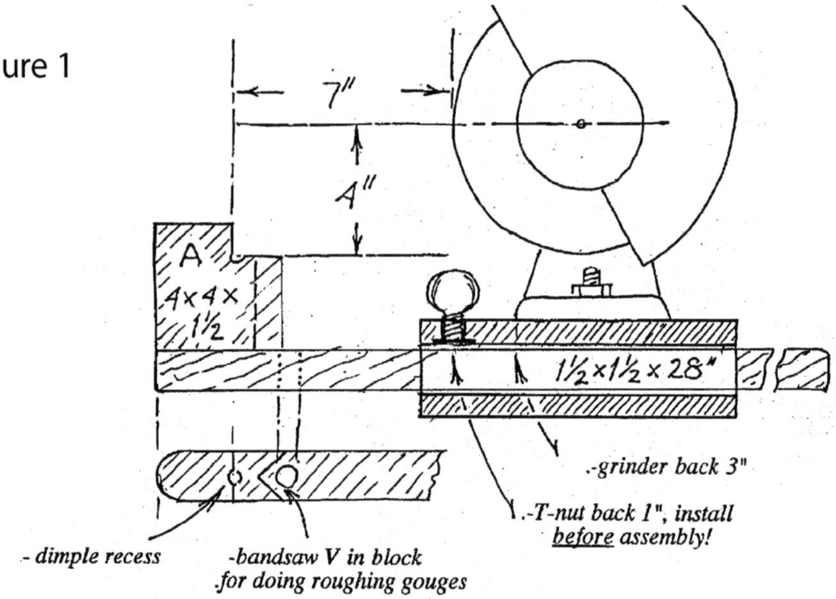


Figure 2

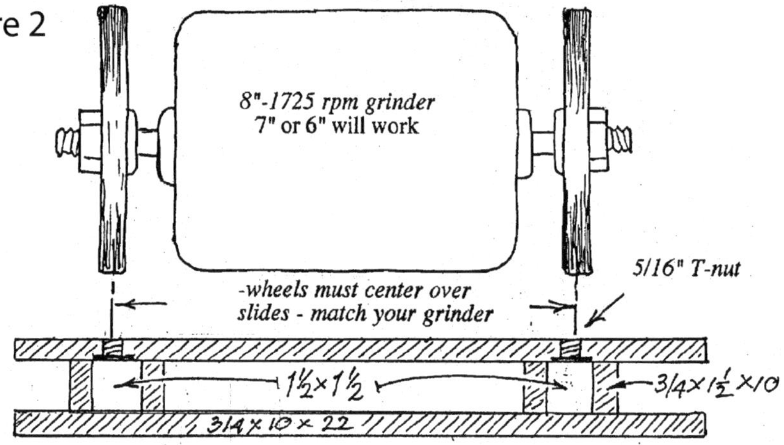


Figure 3

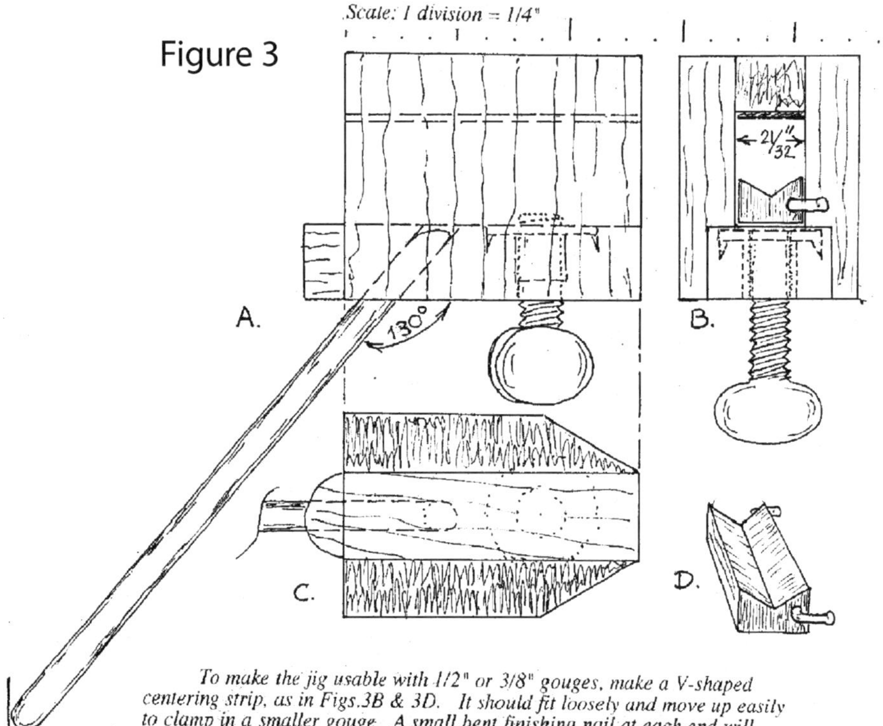


*To make the jig usable with 1/2" or 3/8" gouges, make a V-shaped centering strip, as in Figs.3B & 3D. It should fit loosely and move up easily to clamp in a smaller gouge. A small bent finishing nail at each end will prevent it from falling out. Spray finish as desired.*

Figure 4

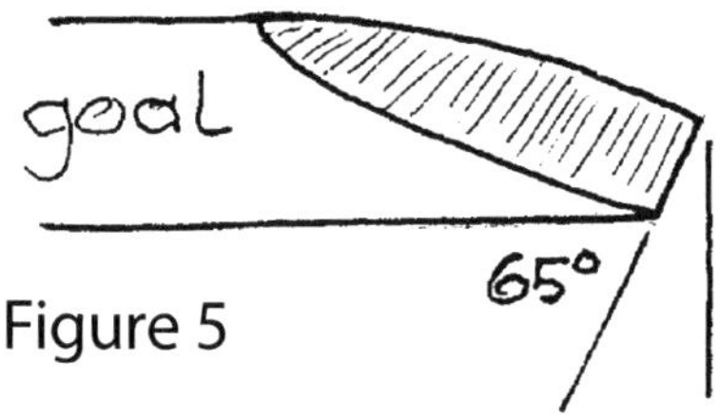


Figure 5

Figure 5, unless it already has one of this angle.

Then turn the tool face down on the wheel and grind off the face of the top at about a 30-degree angle to the long axis, as indicated in the sketches. Continue cautiously until the complete outline of the desired fingernail is seen as in Figure 6. The face will now have flats on each side of the fingernail. These will need to be totally ground away before the tool will be sharp. Note that the sides have much more metal to be ground away than the tip.

Mount your gouge in the 130-degree (50-degree) sharpening jig. The tool should protrude about 2 in. from the face of the jig. It is not necessary to be excessively exact

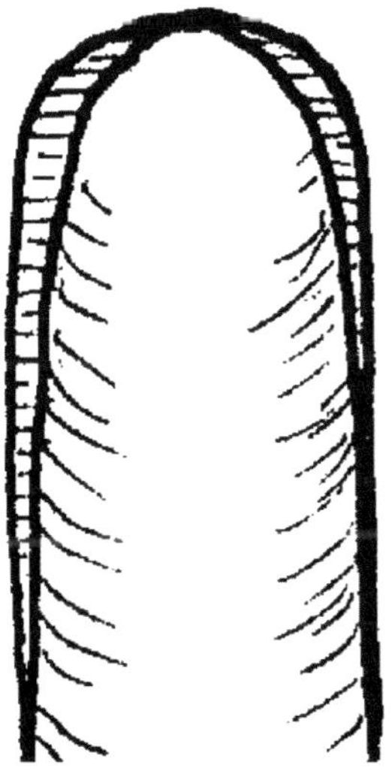

Figure 6

here, but the distance should be the same every time.

Put a distance mark or stop on the base so you can set it the same every time. Set the slide pivot point about 7 in. from the face of the wheel and visually check the nose angle. Adjust to about 65 degrees (or the angle of your choice). As your wheel wears away, you will have to move the slide in slightly to keep the nose bevel grind close to 65 degrees. You can't ignore this factor. I just touch the nose to the stopped wheel and check visually that it is in complete contact with the wheel before starting.

At least 95% of your grinding with a bowl gouge will be on the two sides of the gouge. Skip the tip entirely until the very last pass or two and then keep a light touch as you swing the tip over the wheel. Initially you will not swing the tool handle through enough arc to get the wings ground back properly. The tool handle will have to go through greater than a 180-degree arc, from more than 90 degrees left to more than 90 degrees right, to get the sides of the grind back as in Figure 5. Keep looking at the grind from the side. The two wings should have the same height and contour, and should

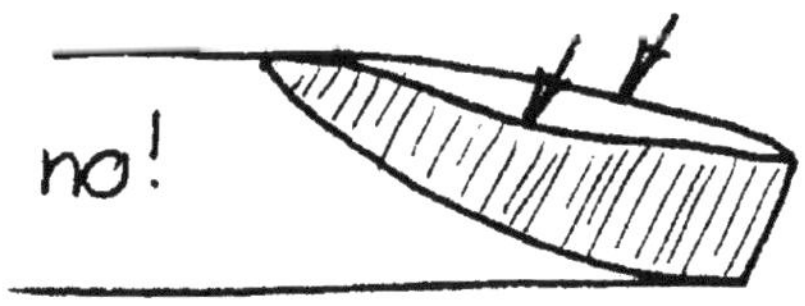


Figure 7

either be flat or slightly convex in profile, not unequal or concave as the near edge of the tool in Figure 7.

In addition, unless you just barely touch the tip of the tool to the wheel as you swing past the midpoint of the arc, the tip will grind back too far and leave two cheeks sticking out ahead of the nose. If this happens you will have to further grind back the wings to eliminate them as they will produce digs and catch in use.

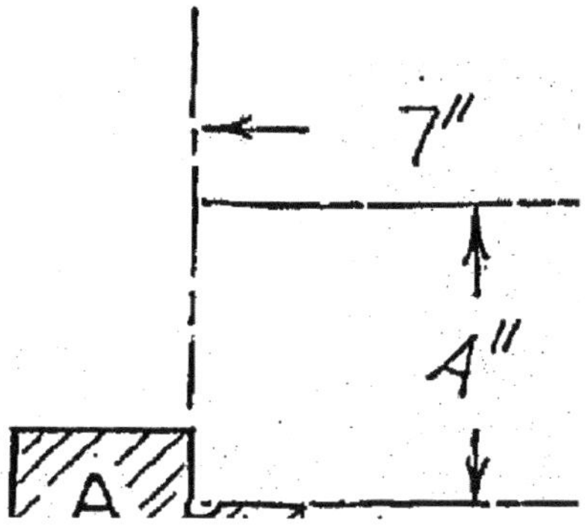


Figure 8

Finally, the jig will also do equally well on a spindle gouge with slight changes in technique. Still leave the tool protrude 2 in. from the face of the jig but move the slide in until the nose angle is about 45 degrees (or your choice). You do not need to grind the top face at all, just start the tool through its full swing on the wheel. The major difference is, in a complete reverse of the bowl gouge, that you will now seem to have to spend most of your grinding time on the tip rather than the sides to avoid having an excessively sharp pointed tool. One smaller 3/8-in. spindle gouge ground this way, however, so that it has a rather pointed fingernail, makes an excellent detailing gouge.

---

*King Heiple is a turner and retired orthopedic surgeon in Pepper Pike, OH. He is a member of the Northcoast Woodturners chapter in Cleveland.*

# Shop-Built Wide-Belt System

*Jim Echter*

While researching sharpening systems for woodturners, belt systems piqued my interest. For years I have been sharpening on an 8" two-wheel dry grinder equipped with a jig for gouges on one wheel, and an adjustable-angle platform for scrapers on the other. But the argument for a flat grind instead of the usual hollow grind made sense to me, so I decided to buy a belt-disk sanding machine and modify it to my purposes.

I possess the frugality gene, which means I needed to find a machine within my limited tool budget. Luckily a couple of members of my local AAW chapter, who also have the frugality gene, discovered that an effective system could be built using an imported belt-disk sander. So off I went to the Harbor Freight store with my 20% off coupon from the Sunday newspaper. I came home with their combination 4" × 36" belt/6" disk sander, catalog number 97181, for about $100 (2013) *(Photo 1)*. The modifications included:

- dismantling the sander table for parts to make a jig-mounting post for gouge sharpening (*Photos 2, 3, 4, 5, 6, 17*)
- extending the disk-sander shaft to mount a buffing wheel for honing (*Photos 7, 11*)
- making and mounting a combo guard and toolrest for the honing wheel (*Photos 8, 9, 10*)
- making an adjustable tool holder for spindle-roughing gouges,

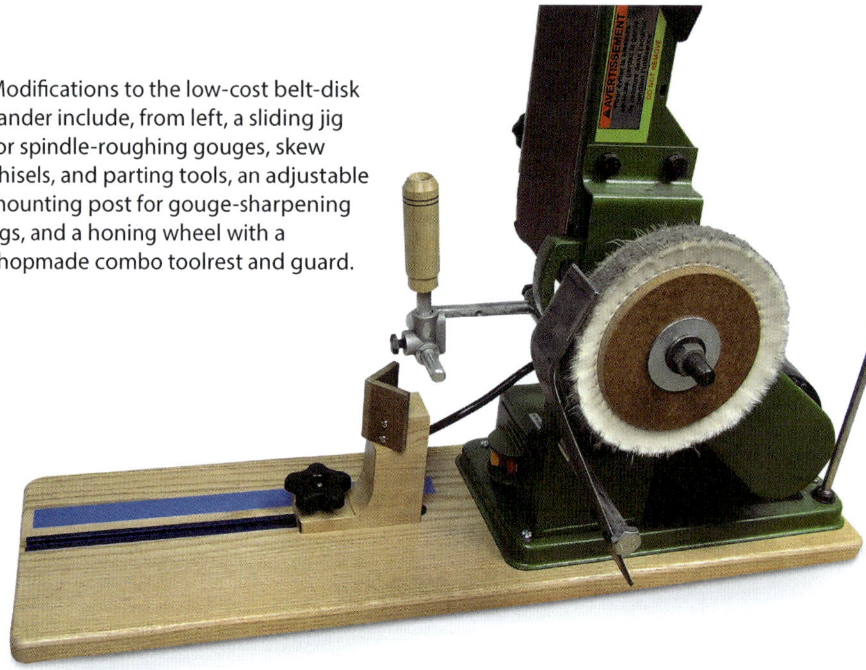

Modifications to the low-cost belt-disk sander include, from left, a sliding jig for spindle-roughing gouges, skew chisels, and parting tools, an adjustable mounting post for gouge-sharpening jigs, and a honing wheel with a shopmade combo toolrest and guard.

**1**

A catalog photo showing the Harbor Freight belt-disk sander fully assembled. Watch for a sale coupon before you buy it.

**2**

For this modification, unpack the parts but do not mount the disk sander or its table. Also, remove the back cover and bottom dust port, the sanding-belt guard, and the drive-belt cover.

AW 27:6, p20

## Jig post and socket

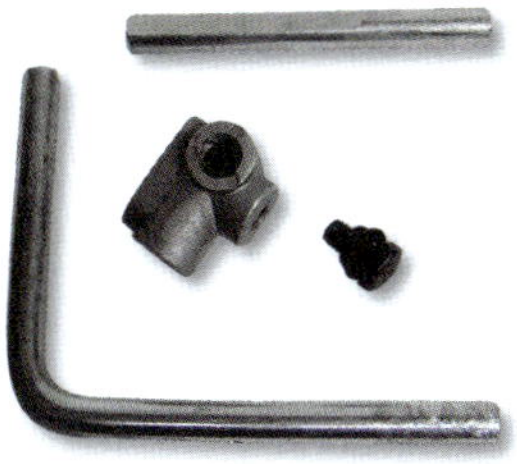

**3**

Dismantle the disk sander's side table and extract these parts, which we used to make a post and socket to hold jigs for the abrasive belt.

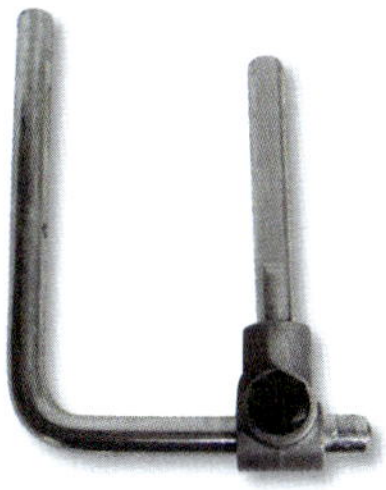

**4**

Assemble the salvaged parts like this.

**5**

(5) Install the parts into the front table hole and tighten the side screw. Between the side screw and the front screw, the post can be positioned to suit the sharpening jig you use.

**6**

Turn a jig socket to slip over the upright post; my post was .470" in diameter so I could drill a 1/2" hole. The jig's ball pivot fits into the socket on top of the turning. *Photo 17* shows how this works.

## Honing disk and guard

**7**

The 1/2" arbor will need a nylon spacer to connect it to the metric disk shaft. Drill out the spacer to match the disk sander side shaft. Drill clearance holes to match the arbor set screws.

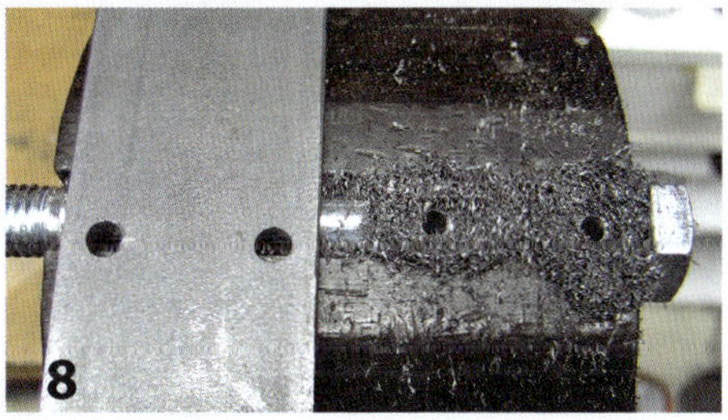

**8**

Use the long bolt and the 1/8" steel bar to make the combo toolrest and guard for the buffing wheel. Drill two 5/32" holes in the mounting bolt. Drill 13/64" clearance holes in the steel bar.

**9**

Tap the 5/32" holes in the bolt for two 10-32 × 1/2" machine screws for mounting the steel guard bar.

**10**

Run the long bolt into the hole in the machine base, then screw the steel bar to it. Bend the bar at 2" for about 30° or what looks right against your wheel.

**11**

To stiffen the buffing wheel, turn a pair of support disks from 1/4" hardboard and back them up with the fender washers. These disks are about 4-1/2" in diameter.

skew chisels, and parting tools *(Photos 12, 13, 16)*

- twisting the drive belt to reverse the direction of the sanding belt and honing wheel *(Photos 14, 15)* With this setup, the belt and disk both run away from the sharp tool edge, eliminating the risk of a dangerous catch. Bowl and spindle gouges can be sharpened in the same manner using the same jigs as you would with grinding wheels. Since the belt runs away from the edge, a quick touch to the buffing wheel, charged with polishing compound, will remove the wire burr. Once you start using this system to sharpen metal tools, never sand wood with it. Wood dust and metal sharpening sparks do not mix. And always remember to wear your safety glasses.

The beauty of this system is that you can change belt grits quickly. Use a coarse-grit belt to change the profile of a tool and a fine-grit belt for putting on a fresh sharp edge. Charge the buffing wheel with an abrasive polishing compound. Just a light touch will remove the wire edge and you are quickly back at the lathe, enjoying the sweetness of a sharp tool.

## Getting started

This system was easy to build. It took longer driving to my local hardware stores to purchase the parts than the actual build time. Listed below are the parts I had to buy, a grand total of about $20 less the arbor, which I already owned.

- One 12 mm × 130 mm bolt
- Two 10-32 × 1/2" machine screws
- One .500 OD × .385 ID × 1" nylon spacer
- One 6" buffing wheel and polishing compound
- One 1/2" arbor
- One 1-1/2" wide × 1/8" thick × 9" long steel bar stock
- Two 1/2" fender washers
- One 8" × 28" hardwood board
- One 12" T-Channel
- One T-Bolt
- One Knob to suit
- Five #8 × 1-1/4" panhead screws for mounting sander to board

---

*Jim Echter is a professional turner who lives near Rochester, NY. He specializes in making tools for fiber artists, turning custom architectural pieces, and teaching. Jim's home club is the Finger Lakes Woodturners Association, and his website is truecreations.biz.*

## Adjustable tool holder

The sliding V block that holds the handle of the tool being sharpened is a piece of 1-1/2" maple with 1/4" hardboard scraps forming the pocket. It slides in a 12" length of T-channel in a routed groove that is centered on the abrasive belt (not on the board).

Drill a 1/4" hole for the T-bolt and plastic locking knob, and drill a second hole near the front for a small piece of 1/4" dowel to help track the V block. Marks on the blue tape index the V block for different tools.

## Reverse direction

To reverse the direction of the sanding belt and honing wheel, loosen the motor bolts and twist the drive belt into a figure eight. Remount the drive-belt cover.

Tighten the motor mount bolts but let the motor twist as much as it can to minimize wear on the twisted belt.

## The machine in action

**16**

Here is the machine in action, sharpening a skew chisel. For easy repeatability, the sliding V block indexes against marks on the blue tape. I removed the rubber feet from the sander and used five #8 x 1-1/4" panhead screws to mount the sander on the wooden base.

**17**

The Tru-Grind gouge-sharpening jig pivots in the socket turned into the top of the jig-holding sleeve.

## Pioneers of belt sharpening *Jon Siegel*

Woodcraft Supply popularized the belt-buff sharpening concept in the 1970s with their Mark II system, which featured a 2" (5 cm) belt running over a large round contact wheel. Today, those machines are collectors' items. When new, they were expensive—$1,400 when corrected for inflation. After using the Woodcraft machine and liking its results, I decided to make my own. It needed to be portable for teaching, to have a flat platen instead of a round contact wheel, an incrementally adjustable pocket jig, and a much lower speed.

*Woodcraft introduced the belt-buff concept 40 years ago with this Mark II system.*

Photo courtesy Guild of New Hampshire Woodworkers

I retained several things from the Woodcraft design: a five-second belt change, pocket jigs instead of a platform, the ability to sharpen and buff on the same machine, and upward belt travel, away from the edge. This quest led me to converting low-cost imported 4" × 36" (10 cm × 90 cm) belt sanders. I sold more than 200 through my company, Big Tree Tools LLC.

In 2012, we decided to stop making the machines. Woodworkers continued to ask about them, however, and I reconsidered how I could further the belt-sharpening revolution. I have assembled a team to design a new and better belt machine that will be capable of sharpening most woodworking hand tools. Having already built hundreds of the previous models, we have good ideas about what we need to improve.

*On the Big Tree Tools flat-platen belt machine, both sides of a skew chisel can be ground and sharpened from a single jig position. The belt machine works equally well if the edge of the skew is straight or curved.*

### Advantages of a belt machine

Converting woodworkers from wheels to belts involves big changes, but the advantages are huge:

- Grinding wheels run too fast, overheating the steel, intimidating beginners, and sometimes causing accidents.
- It is time-consuming to change the grit in a grinder wheel system; turners will settle for using the same grit for everything, which limits versatility. Belts can be changed in five seconds.
- With a belt-buff system, chisels can be sharpened in ten seconds (including setup and deburring). This eliminates sharpening procrastination and fosters turning with truly sharp tools.
- A belt-buff system virtually eliminates time-consuming hand-honing, while accurate jigs assure repeatable setups that allow you to remove the minimum amount of metal.

To get started before our new machines are ready for market, consider following our approach, as developed by Jim Echter in his DYI belt-sharpening system article. You will be delighted to have evolved beyond the stone age of sharpening.

Jon Siegel can be contacted at big@proctornet.com.

# Does Honing Pay Off?

*Alan Lacer & Jeryl Wright*

I have heard many discussions and fielded a lot of interesting questions while traveling amongst woodturners. A common assertion is that some steels don't get as sharp as others or that high carbon steel (HCS) tools get much sharper than high speed steel (HSS) tools. Another common view is that honing is a waste of time: the burr will "strop off" in the wood; honing takes so much time it's inefficient; or woodturners don't need a really sharp tool. Often, such views about steel and honing are spoken as fact, not just opinion. My experiences run counter to these viewpoints, so I knew something more was needed to test these "facts" in an objective, scientific manner.

How do you test for sharpness? There are tests used in the cutlery trade to measure the amount of force needed to cut rubber bands or to measure a knife's penetration into various objects. While this can be an easy test for a flat knife blade, testing for sharpness is a bit harder to do with gouges and thick skew chisels. With the help of Jerry Wright, I decided to conduct empirical sharpening and turning tests and let readers judge which sharpening methods produce the best turned surface. Images of highly magnified cutting edges and turned surfaces are provided as objective data. From these images one can judge the degree of sharpness of an edge and the impact that edge has on a piece of wood, cut in the way a woodturner would be using the tool. The surface finish that a tool creates on wood has significance: Does one need to start with 40-grit abrasive or is sanding even needed, a decision that will have an impact on the turned object's shape and detail, amount of dust produced, surface finish, and time spent sanding.

## Tool preparation

We tested skew chisels and bowl gouges from major tool manufacturers. First, we ground the edges using a dry wheel grinder, adhering to standard methods of sharpening. We ground them freehand, using a rigid platform for support. The grinder ran at 1,725 rpm and had a 60 grit SG, 8"-diameter wheel. Grinding was

### Methods of honing

To place the bevel of a skew chisel correctly on a diamond hone, hold the handle securely and use an up-and-down motion, starting at the back of the bevel. Move the hone to simultaneously touch the area just below the cutting edge and the back of the bevel.

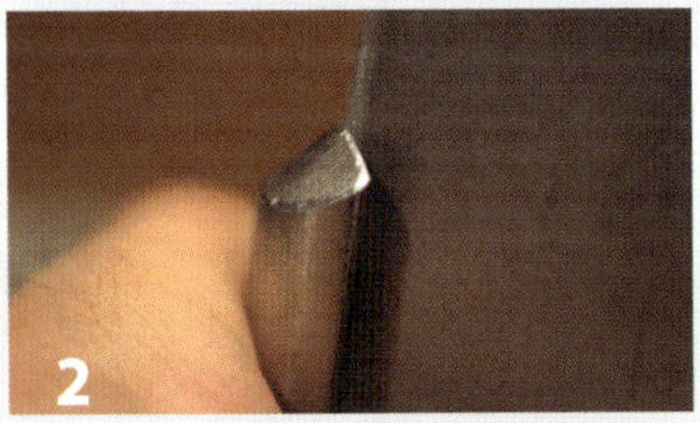


The flute of a gouge must also be honed. The curved radius of a slipstone or a tapered diamond cone is held flat in the flute and worked with a back-and-forth motion.

### Polishing flutes

To polish or refine the flute of a gouge, use a wheel made of MDF, turned to a convex shape that fits the profile of the flute. Coat the wheel with an emery stick. Work only the last 1" or so of the flute. The wheel should spin away from you.

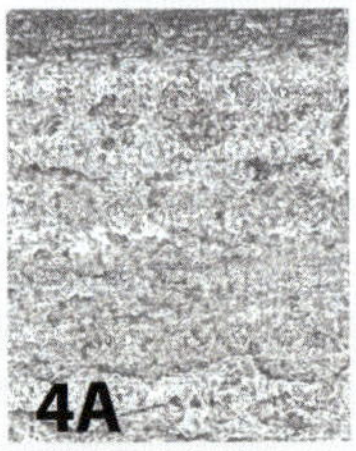


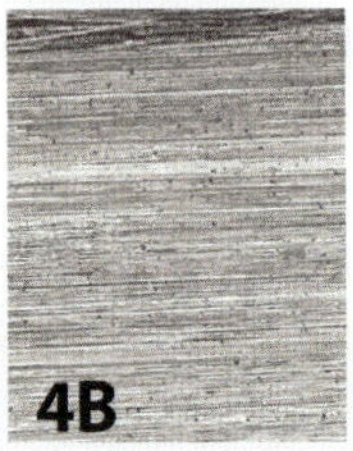


(4A) Gouge flute with milling marks (100X).

(4B) Gouge flute after polishing (100X).

AW 24:2, p22

## Polishing flutes: progression of honing and polishing

Gouge edge, ground only (20X).

Gouge edge, bevel honed (20X).

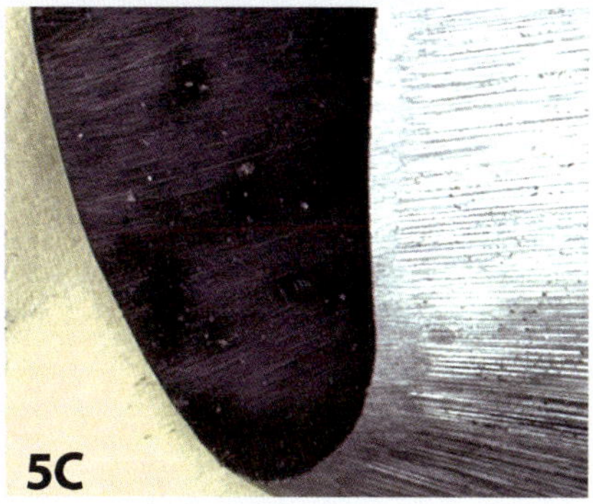

(5C) Gouge edge, bevel and flute honed (20X).

(5D) Gouge edge, bevel honed, flute honed and polished (100X).

conducted until the sparks came evenly over the top of the tool's edge. For each tool's bevel, we produced a single facet, slightly hollow ground. Bevel angles were uniform from tool to tool.

## Methods of honing

We honed the bevels of the skews and gouges with the flat side of a 600-grit, diamond slipstone and used the curved edges of the slipstone to hone the inside flutes of the gouges. A flat hone for the skews and the outside bevel of gouges, combined with a tapered diamond hone for the flutes of gouges, would have worked equally well. To avoid rounded over cutting edges, we maintained a two-point contact of the bevels (hone touching at the back of bevel and just below the cutting edge). When honing the inside of gouges, we held the rounded edge of the hone flat inside the flute. For tools freshly ground, the honing process took under three minutes. Less than one minute is normal for honing between grinding. *(Photos 1 and 2)*

## Polishing flutes

We polished the flute of one of the gouges to determine if this additional preparation had any impact on the sharpness. To polish the flute, we turned a disc of medium density fiberboard (MDF) and then created a bead to fit the profile of the flute. The MDF can be mounted on a faceplate or an arbor as shown in *Photo 3*. (Either work from the back of the lathe, or if you intend to run the lathe in reverse, secure the faceplate or arbor to the spindle.) With the direction of rotation spinning away from you, charge the bead area with a stick of emery. We polished only the last 1" of the flute to remove the milling marks. Depending on the hardness and toughness of the steel, this usually takes less than five minutes. *(Photos 4A and 4B)*

The cutting edges of gouges are shown as they are refined from an initial ground state through the progression of honing and polishing. Note the removal of grinding burrs. *(Photos 5A-5D)*

Cutting edges of skew chisels are shown as they are refined from the ground state to the honed state. Note the reduction of edge roughness after honing. *(Photos 6A-6D)*

## Methods of cutting wood

To provide a challlenge, we chose dried redwood (8% moisture content) for our tests, since it's not particularly desirable for turning. To test the gouges, we mounted the wood on a screw chuck, grain orientated as for bowl turning. When testing the skew chisels, the wood was mounted between centers, grain direction parallel to the axis of the lathe. Bowl gouge cuts were from smaller to larger diameters, with the flute pointed in the direction of cut. This is a common method of using a bowl gouge and never approached a finishing-type method of cutting.

## Wood cutting basics

Much has been written about the process of chip formation and resulting wood surfaces, because of its importance to commercial wood processing. The most important variables affecting milled or planed wood surfaces (other than wood species, moisture content, and grain orientation) are cutter velocity, feed rate, depth of cut, and cutting edge sharpness. Higher cutter rpm, slower feed rate, shallower cuts, and higher degrees of sharpness all improve surface finish. Within the limits available to woodturners, tool sharpness is the strongest variable. It has been shown in commercial

## Polishing flutes: edges of skew chisels

Skew chisel edge, bevel ground only (20X).

Skew chisel edge, ground and honed (20X).

Edge view of skew chisel edge, ground (200X).

Edge view of skew chisel, ground and honed (200X).

milling operations that very minor improvements in cutting edge sharpness cause fourfold reductions in surface roughness.

Cutting edges are formed by the intersection of two surfaces. The refinement of the cutting edge determines its sharpness. Intersections of rough surfaces create blunt or jagged edges while intersections of smooth surfaces create sharp edges. This is commonly accepted for those familiar with chisels, plane irons, and knives. It is routine to bring these linear edges to high degrees of refinement using a series of stones of increasing fineness. On the other hand, woodturning tools can have complex, curved shapes, often ground from two sides. Admittedly, these edges can be difficult to grind and hone.

## Grinding wheels

With the advent of modern HSS and high-wear steels for turning tools, choosing the right grinding wheel is a must. First of all, gray wheels are out. They grind slowly or hardly at all, require constant dressing, go dull quickly, and generate too much heat. A premium friable aluminum oxide wheel in 60 or 80 grit for sharpening and 46 grit for heavy grinding in an I, J, or K hardness (I is the softest, K harder, and J is my preferred choice) will work well. Expect to pay between $45 and $75 each for an 8" quality wheel.

The newer seeded gel (SG) wheels work even better and have a longer life. Constructed of submicron crystalline particles that constantly reveal sharp edges, these wheels grind aggressively and have a long life. The Norton Company produces a high-end 8" version and a new line of 3X wheels. They perform quite well. The less expensive wheels do not have as high a percentage of the crystalline material as the premium wheels, yet they grind well on modern tools.

Regardless of the type of grinding wheel you use, you *must* regularly dress it to clean, sharpen, level, and true it. For SG wheels, a diamond dresser is a must, but diamond dressers also work great on any wheel. Avoid the cheaply made plated wheel dressers, opting for either a jigging system with one large diamond or a T-shaped system for freehand dressing. Dressing grinding wheels frequently and lightly keeps them in top shape.

## Hardness of materials

To see why traditional hones and grinding wheels may have trouble with HSS and high-wear steels, compare the different hardness values below. All HSS and high-wear steels contain significant quantities of vanadium carbides, which exceed the hardness of many abrasives.

**Relative Knoop hardness values:**

- Diamond = 7000 to 8000
- Cubic boron nitride (CBN) = 4700
- Vanadium carbide = 2500
- Silicon carbide = 2400
- Aluminum oxide = 2100
- Tungsten carbide = 1900
- Hardened steel (65 HRC) = 825
- Quartz (silica) = 700 (Arkansas and Washita stones are classified as silica-quartz.)

## Methods of examination

The variously sharpened skews and gouges and turned redwood were examined and photographed using a 54 megapixel optical imaging microscope, at magnifications up to 200X. The field of view at this magnification is approximately 3/64" wide. This high magnification, unusually high depth of field, and color photography make possible the easy observation of the cutting edges and the relative smoothness of the cut surfaces.

## Gouges: effects of grinding and honing

Gouges manufactured from M2 HSS were chosen to demonstrate the impact of different edge-preparation methods on the appearance of the cutting edge as well as the appearance of the cut wood surfaces. Then gouges manufactured from 2030, 2060, CPM 10V (A11) and CPM 15V were chosen to determine whether fine-edge preparation techniques would be successful on these highly alloyed steels.

We prepared the gouges to test three ways: only the bevel ground, the bevel ground and honed, and the bevel ground and honed and the flute honed. Photos 7A, 7B, 8A, 8B, 9A and 9B show the progression of edges from coarse to refined as the burrs are removed by honing, as well as improvement in cut-wood surfaces. The edges become smoother as the intersecting surfaces become more refined. As a result, there is a huge difference in wood surfaces cut with a gouge that was only ground and one that was ground and honed. *(Photo 10)*

Results from the highly alloyed materials are shown in *Photos 11A-11D*. We also noted that similar results are possible with 2030, 2060, CPM 10V (A11) and CPM 15V, grades that are often thought to be difficult or impossible to sharpen.

## Skews: effects of grinding and honing

Skews manufactured from M2 HSS were chosen to demonstrate the impact of different edge-preparation methods on the appearance of the cutting edge as well as the appearance of the cut wood surfaces. We then chose skews manufactured from PM (powdered metal) M4, 2060, and CPM (Crucible Particle Metallurgy) 10V (A11) to determine whether fine-edge preparation techniques would be successful on these highly alloyed steels. A skew chisel made from HCS was also examined to judge the edge quality versus the base M2. Often, it is thought that HCS can produce a better edge.

Skews are deceptively difficult to sharpen. The cutting edge is the intersection of two ground surfaces. The relative coarseness of each surface has a decided impact on the edge as the surfaces interact with each other. As a result, the fineness of the grinds directly affects the edge sharpness.

Skews were prepared two ways: bevel ground and bevel ground and honed. Photos 12A, 12B, 13A and 13B show the edges of the skew and the cutting results of the wood's surface, using an M2 skew, ground and ground and honed. The cut wood surfaces show a marked difference from rough and torn, to much more level and uniform.

The results we received from HCS, as well as highly alloyed materials, demonstrate that similar results are also possible with low alloy HCS as well as PM M4, 2060, and CPM 10V (A11), again, grades that are often thought to be difficult or impossible to sharpen.

## Gouges: effects of grinding and honing

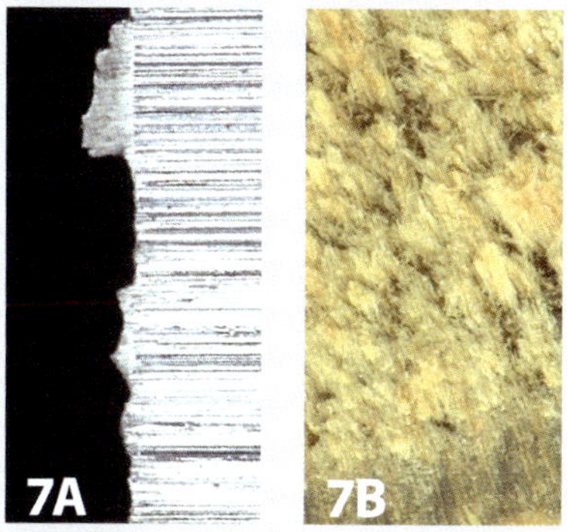


(7A) Cutting edge of a M2 HSS gouge, ground only (200X).

(7B) Resulting cut wood surface (100X).

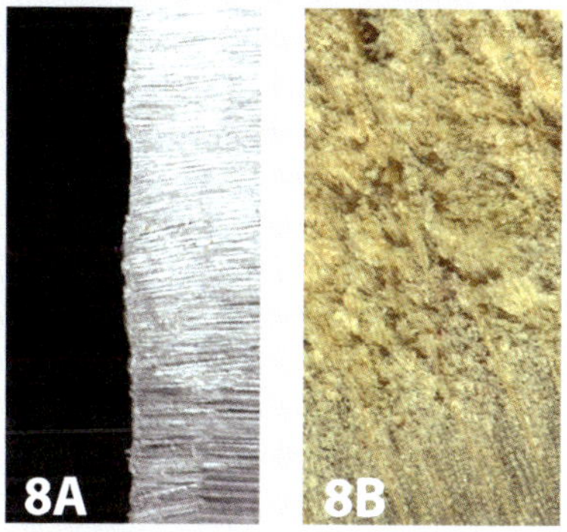


(8A) Cutting edge of a M2 HSS gouge, bevel ground and honed (200X).

(8B) Resulting cut wood surface (100X).

(9A) Cutting edge of a M2 HSS gouge, bevel and flute honed (200X).

(9B) Resulting cut wood surface (100X).

## Gouge comparison

Even with an unmagnified view, huge differences are observable in surface finishes. The upper half was cut with a freshly ground M2 bowl gouge, while the lower half was cut with a 2060 bowl gouge, bevel and flute honed.

## Effects of gouges

Magnification 100X, wood surfaces cut with PM 2030 gouge.

Magnification 100X, wood surfaces cut with PM 2060 gouge.

Magnification 100X, wood surfaces cut with CPM 10V gouge.

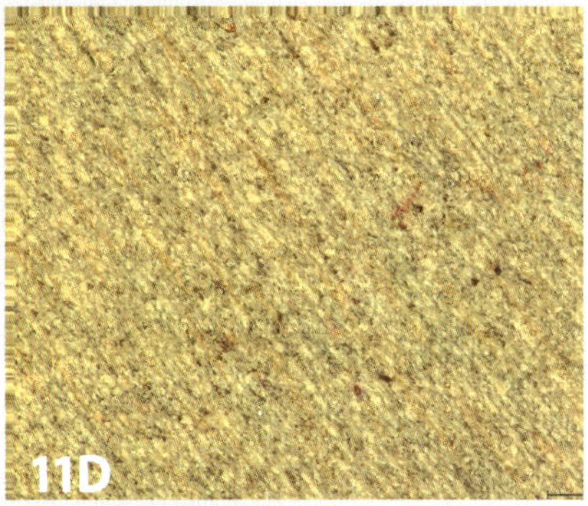


Magnification 100X, wood surfaces cut with CPM 15V gouge.

## Observations

From a woodturner's perspective, there are a number of conclusions to be drawn from the examination of tool edges and the wood cut with those edges.

- All of the different steels got sufficiently sharp to cut the wood cleanly and that is what it's really all about, rather than some mystical concept of sharpness. The method of preparing the edge is the key to tool sharpness. Clearly, an edge that is not honed produces a torn surface when cutting poor-quality wood, regardless of the steel. Some woodturners believe that there is no need to hone, as the burr will simply strop off in the wood; however, experience with HSS and especially the higher wearing steels (10V, 2030, 2060, 15V) is that the burr is tough and does not readily strop off in the wood.
- Diamond honing materials can easily cut all of the steel alloys on the market. Traditional stones (Arkansas, Washita, India, crysolon, ceramic) are ineffective or require an inordinate amount of time to achieve an improved edge on HSS and also on the high-wear steels we tested. This is because the common HSS, like M2 and M4, super HSS such as PM 2030 and 2060, and the high-wear steels such as CPM 10V and 15V, contain significant quantities of hard carbides. These tungsten, molybdenum, and vanadium carbides far exceed the hardness of traditional sharpening stones. Jerry Glaser, who championed the use of highly alloyed PM materials, referred to traditional honing materials as "old methods" and diamond as "new methods" of honing—we have

## Skews: effects of grinding and honing

Cutting edge of a M2 HSS skew, ground (200X).

Resulting cut wood surface (100X).

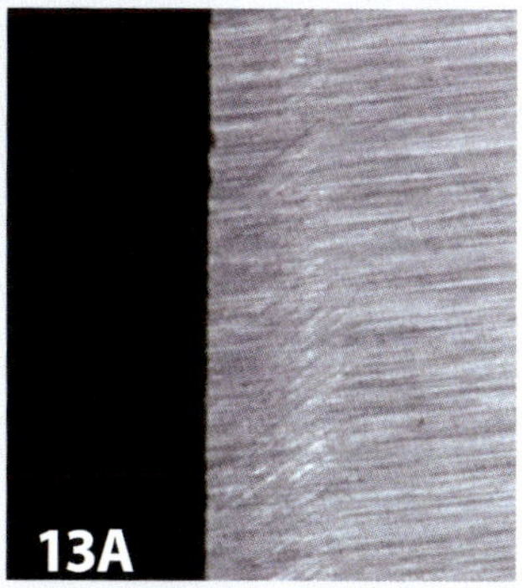

Cutting edge of a M2 HSS skew, ground and honed (200X).

Resulting cut wood surface (100X).

to learn to work with diamond. All of the different types of diamond (synthetic mono and polycrystalline, as well as natural) on the market will hone contemporary turning tools. However, the type of diamond, smoothness of plate, and how diamond is attached to a plate determine the longevity of a diamond hone.

- A cutting edge is the intersection of two planes—and both of those planes should be smooth to produce a fine edge. On skew chisels, this is not an issue once you have honed both surfaces. However, with gouges, the bevel is produced by grinding and honing, while the inside surface is a product of the manufacturing process. Honing does smooth inner flutes when done with a slipstone or cone, but for those who don't hone, or those with flutes that have very deep grooves from the milling process, there is a problem of sharpness.
- A well-manufactured flute, free of deep milling marks, is a big plus and can speed the honing process. Polishing the flutes is an option, but it would be admirable if was already done by the tool makers. Honing with diamond will, to a large extent, cut through most of the milling marks sooner or later, so polishing may not offer a huge increase in edge sharpness over regular honing.

To be fair to all of those who have argued that honing is a waste of time or that certain steels do not get as sharp as others, it seems as though those viewpoints are based on the honing material being used. Traditional honing materials work well on HCS tools but poorly, slowly, or virtually not at all on HSS and high-wear steels, so if you don't hone HSS and high-wear steel with a diamond hone, they will not be as sharp as HCS that has been honed.

---

*Alan Lacer (www.alanlacer.com) is a woodturner, teacher, and writer living near River Falls, WI. Dr. Jeryl Wright (jeryl.wright@crucible.com) is a woodturner and vice president of technology for Crucible Specialty Metals in Syracuse, NY. He earned a ScD in metallurgy from Massachusetts Institute of Technology.*

# How to Hone Edge Tools

*Alan Lacer*

For me honing is like a cold swim-quickly in and quickly out. The honing process should be under 45 seconds in most situations-even with a large tool like a roughing gouge. If it takes longer, then either I have a poor honing technique or the edge is past the point of being honable. Then it's back to the grinder.

Shaping the tool and grinding properly are fundamental and are more critical than honing. You can't hone a poorly ground tool and it's a complete waste of time to hone unless you've performed these other steps well.

Assuming you have acquired a serviceable shape for the task, grind the tool to a level where honing will both be possible and beneficial to the turning process. Here's what works for me: Aim for slight hollow-ground bevels and minimal facets-especially facets above the concave face of the hollow-ground bevel.

## Why hollow-ground bevels work best

Why a hollow-ground, why not a flat or convex bevel? The only reason I see for the hollow- ground bevel is that it provides a built-in honing guide. As long as there is a two-point contact surface, I can better feel the honing process (see illustrations). However, there must be a balance between too much and too little hollow grinding. I prefer the concave profile a 6" to 8" diameter wheel produces. A smaller-diameter wheel produces such a deep hollow that it may weaken the edge; a larger diameter produces almost no hollow and is more difficult to hone.

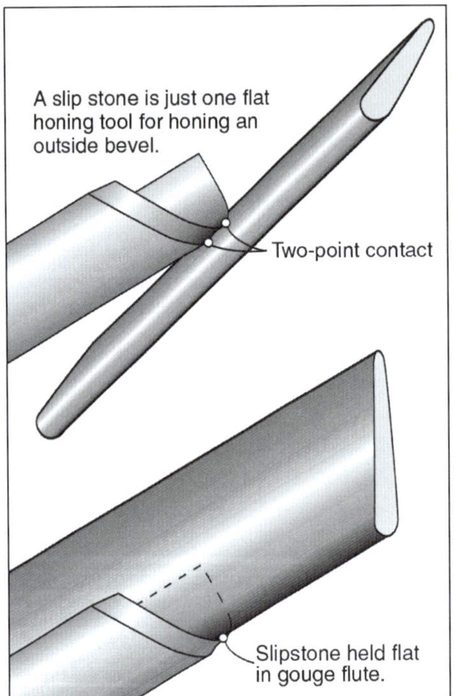

A slipstone (shown), round, or tapered rod or cone works effectively to hone an inside flute.

Producing a ground surface with minimal facets is essential. If there are multi-facets that arise above the line from the heel of the bevel to the cutting edge, then you'll be honing only the high points and not refining or improving your edge. Just as in grinding the edge, I train myself not to hone the edge - focus on the bevel. If you focus on the edge, invariably you'll grind a short bevel just behind the cutting edge. Or when honing, you'll dub or rollover the edge.

When we talk of honing there are usually two ways to understand it: hand-honing and power-honing. When hand-honing, you use a stone, rubberized abrasive or piece of leather. Among turners, some type of stone is most common.

## The proper stone

First, select a suitable stone. I've had the best luck honing contemporary tool steels with the man-made India slipstone in a medium grit and, of course, with diamond (fine and super fine). Technically the India stone is an oilstone, but I tend to use them dry and regularly clean the build-up of metal particles with WD-40. The India slip is fine for removing burrs from the inside of gouges and the flat side functions to hone the outside bevel of gouges. However, in a short time the flat side becomes concave and does not work so well for skews and parting tools. It is still okay for gouges, but not for the flat tools.

For flat tools (and an occasional outside bevel of gouges and ring/hook type tools) I prefer a diamond-coated stone (usually diamond applied to a mild steel plate). For gouge flutes, the diamond-tapered rod or cone works quite well. Be careful with diamond-coated systems, as not all are of

AW 18:1, p50

the same quality. Cheaper stones often incorporate fewer diamond particles or a type of industrial diamond that breaks down quickly. My caution: You get what you pay for.

## Honing technique

I have seen many variations of honing techniques:

1. Fixing the honing stone to a flat surface and working the tool back and forth along the stone.

2. Bracing the tool against the tailstock lock and moving the stone along the edge (tool is stationary).

3. Placing the butt end of the handle firmly upright on a bench or the lathe stand and moving the stone along the tool.

I prefer to stand solidly with the tool against my body, then, move the stone along the tool.

As for the actual honing process, I always begin at the heel of the ground bevel. Next, I start the action of honing with a back and forth motion from the heel towards the edge. When I feel the bevel adequately I lower this honing action towards the cutting edge until I feel that second point of contact. Always maintain this two-point contact with the hone bridging the slight concave region between the heel of the bevel and the area just below the cutting edge. Remember, you are honing the bevel and not the edge.

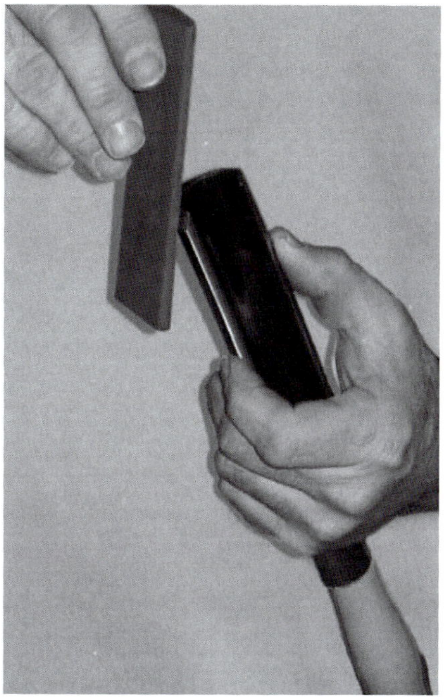

When honing, support the turning tool handle solidly against the body. The grip shown keeps the tool stationary.

If the tool is a gouge or hook/ring type of tool, I finish by honing the inside flute. The nicety of this last operation, at least with gouges, is that I have another built-in honing guide: hold the slipstone or rounded rod flat in the flute, not touching the edge itself, but focusing on the two planes that trap the area we call the edge.

There is another approach that can be used in combination with hand-honing or as a substitute for it: power-honing. This is most often done with a motorized wheel or a wheel mounted on a lathe arbor. Wheel materials include felt, stitched cotton, leather, cardboard, rubberized abrasive, plywood, and MDF. For turning tools, I tend to stay away from the softer surfaces (felt, leather, cloth and cardboard). With our heavy-weight tools and too much pressure, a soft wheel runs the risk of rolling over the edge. My first choice is also a frugal one: medium density fiberboard (MDF) charged with a buffing compound that cuts high-speed steel.

## MDF wheel

You can glue up the MDF wheel from discarded cutoff scraps from a cabinet shop. I make the wheel diameter approximately the size

## Honing Strategies

**Gouges:** Hone the outside bevel. Then hone the inside flute with a slipstone, round rod, or cone.

**Skews:** Hone four faces on these tools: the two ground bevels (be- gin here), the top edge that will refine the long point, and the bottom edge that will refine the short point.

**Parting tools:** Use a flat hone to work both ground sides. On thin-kerf parting tools, hone the flat sides to refine the corners.

**Ring/hook tools:** These come two ways, ground bevel inside, and ground bevel outside. On both styles, work the outside surface with a flat hone. If the ground bevel is outside, work the inside of a hook tool with a narrow slipstone. Choose a round honing rod for ring tools. If the inside is ground, a tapered or round stone in a drill are favorites, hand-hone the surface with the same stone used for grinding.

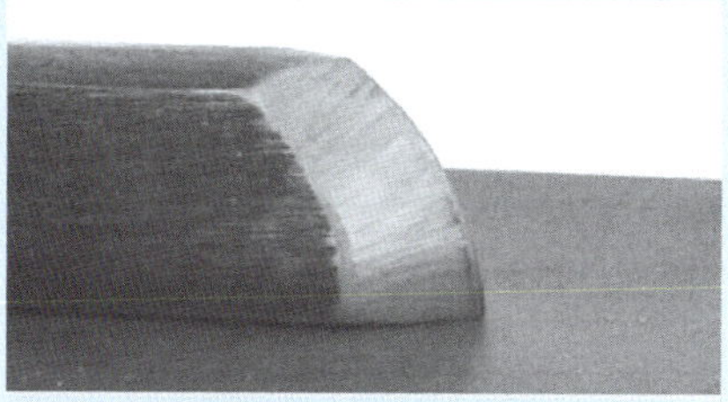

*Skews have four surfaces to hone: two ground bevels and two side edges that define he short and long points.*

of the grinding wheels in my shop so that the hollow ground area is simpler to feel. Since I grind on an 8-in. wheel grinder, my MDF flat wheels are 7 in. to 7-1/2 in. in diameter and 1-1/2 in. wide (two 3/4-in. pieces glued together). I mount the wheel on an arbor and turn the wheel to a round flat disc.

Here are some suggestions to mount your disc: arbor-mounted directly onto a 1/4 hp or 1/3 hp 1725 rpm motor; pillow block and shaft, or left on an arbor that mounts on the lathe. It's best to avoid mounting the wheel on the lathe you'll be working on, as it is not practical to remove work from the lathe to hone.

Whatever system you choose, set up to hone with the wheel turning away from you. Remember, honing is quick operation. I find that high speed is not necessary. I prefer 600 rpm to 1,000 rpm.

Choose a buffing compound rated for stainless steel. I've had great luck with the Dico brand and Zam, a green honing compound. Whatever you use, watch for the honing compound to turn black as you hone. This indicates that you are removing some metal and not simply polishing the tool surface.

Stop power-honing when you see a mud trail at an MDF wheel charged with honing compound.

## Techniques at the wheel

The power technique is straightforward and similar to hand honing. With the wheel moving away from you, charge it with honing compound, place the heel of the bevel towards the top of the wheel, cutting edge up.

Gently lower the bevel onto the wheel until you have that same two-point or full contact of the bevel on the wheel. Do not focus on the edge, because you will round it over in a nano-second. When I see the blackened mud trail just coming under the edge, I stop.

Power-honing is a quick process. If-a-little-is-good-more-must-be-great is the wrong approach.

Personally, the only tool I routinely power-hone is the skew chisel, its long edge benefits from this treatment. Occasionally I power-hone the outside bevel of gouges when I have a particularly difficult piece of wood. In that case I either use the slipstone to hone the inside flute, or I have MDF wheels with turned beads that fit the inside flute of the gouges.

---

*Alan Lacer (AlanLacer.com) is a woodturner, teacher, and writer living near River Falls, WI.*

# Scraper Sharpness

*Alan Lacer & Jeryl Wright*

A woodturner's scraper can remove wood with the brute force of a bulldozer or the finesse of a barber's razor. This flexibility parallels that of the furniture- or cabinetmaker's scraper.

Such craftspeople know that their scrapers can remove planer marks and dried glue or leave a finish on wood superior to sandpaper. In skilled hands, a scraper can even level a cured finish. These broad abilities are all the result of the way in which the scraper is sharpened and presented.

The woodturner's scraper is a relative newcomer in our field. Turning scrapers made their widespread appearance in general woodturning after the introduction of electric motors to power the lathe. Unless a turner worked on a small scale and/or in dense hardwoods or ivory, it was difficult to remove wood with a scraping action on human-powered lathes.

Scrapers have been popular in the patternmaking trade and with students in shop classes. In patternmaking, they were often a favorite for creating specific shapes with close tolerances, where clean cuts were not always the object (torn grain could be filled and sanded).

In some school settings, scrapers were the only tools, as gouges and skew chisels demanded more skill. The shop teacher required a higher level of woodturning skill to teach such tools, and scrapers were often thought to be a safer alternative.

AW 23:4, p46

## Scraping vs. cutting

What makes a tool a scraper? It is not really the name of the tool, as one can "cut" with a scraper and "scrape" with a cutting tool such as a skew chisel.

The answer lies in presentation angle. Like the cabinetmaker's scraper, the tool is presented to the wood with no bevel supporting the edge, only the wood passing over the edge.

In a cutting action, the edge has some support of the bevel area to essentially lever away the wood, rather than scrape it off. Think of the difference between scraping off the skin of an orange with just the edge of a knife versus coming in at a low angle to peel away the skin. Or, closer to woodturning: Try grabbing a carving tool or bench chisel and presenting it in such a way as to scrape off the wood with just the edge, versus attacking it at a lower angle, using the bevel as a fulcrum to start cutting away the wood. Finally, most turners' scrapers are made from flat stock with only one side ground (unlike a parting tool or skew chisel).

Specific applications often dictate how scrapers are used. Early English turning books taught the mantra that "wood prefers to be cut rather than scraped." Although generally true, here are situations where a scraper is extremely useful:

- when the surface finish does not matter (facing off the outside bottom of a bowl for a faceplate or chuck or roughing the inside of a lidded box);

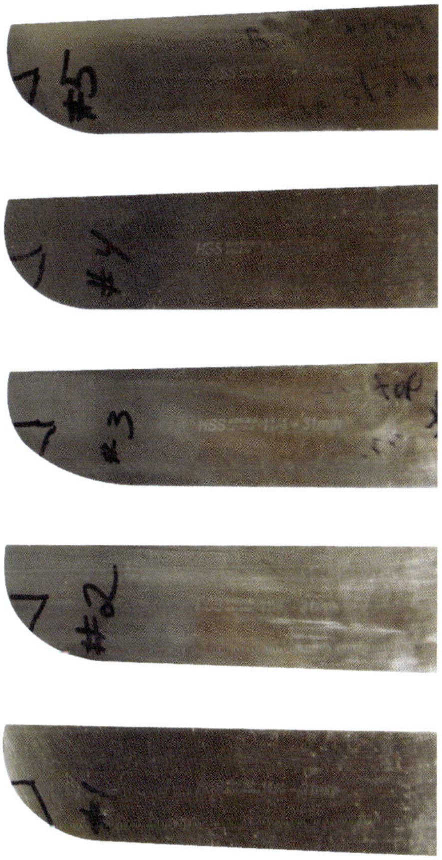


- when sacrificing a burr rather than a sharp edge is preferable (working bark, glue, or dirt when rough-shaping a piece);
- when a safer approach than a cutting tool is required (in aggressive areas on bowls, hollow turning);
- when leveling or blending a surface (inside bottom of a bowl or the large face of a plate or platter); or
- when a fine-finishing tool is required (leveling a finish).

## Preparing new scrapers

A new scraper needs a considerable bit of tuning. First, the sharp corners behind the cutting edge require softening. Some tools come sharp enough on these edges to cut flesh—and tear up tool rests or drag on the rest. A belt sander is the easiest tool with which to soften these edges.

Second, the top surface is often an abysmal surface either because of pitted steel or deep milling marks. In the worst cases, use a belt sander/grinder with a flat platen to remove the marks. To remedy less-severe factory marks, polish the top surface (polish only the first 1" to 2" with a 600-grit or finer diamond hone, WD-40, and a little elbow grease).

As for shape, the beauty of a scraper is that the shape is whatever you need or desire. For most applications, a French curve or side radius (only the left side) performs well. For the bevel angle (actually a relief angle on scrapers), 20 to 40 degrees off 90 degrees (most turners would call this a 50- to 70-degree angle) works well.

When you buy scrapers, the factory grind often has a minimal relief angle. We do not want this bevel to contact the wood—it can inadvertently produce a horrendous dig-in.

Rather than grinding scrapers to a negative-rake angle, grind a greater relief angle. Most negative-rake scrapers also arrive with a grinder-produced top surface—not well polished.

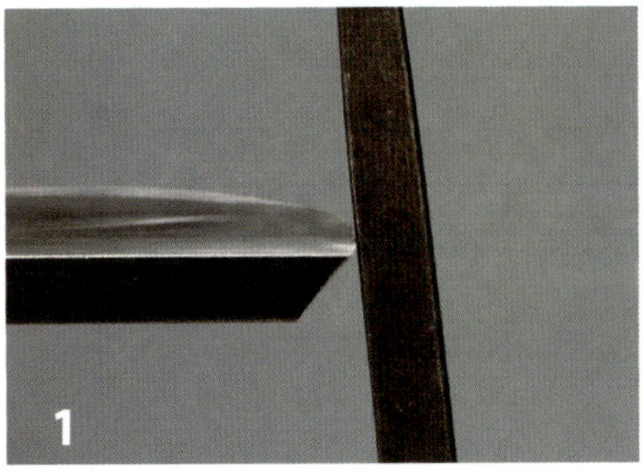

1

To pull a burr with a burnisher or a diamond hone, steady the tool and present the burnisher (triangular, oval, or round) at a 3- to 5-degree tilt toward the top of the tool. Make one steady pass. The amount of pressure you apply changes the burr from light to heavy.

2

In "normal" scraping, the tool is held flat on the tool rest (positioned close to the work) with the handle raised slightly in back and with only the edge contacting the wood.

3

A finishing technique to remove small amounts of wood is often called "shear scraping." The tool is no longer flat on the rest but canted in the direction of the cut at around a 45- to 70-degree angle.

## Develop the edge

The key to preparing the scraper is developing a feel for burrs. Every skilled cabinet- or furnituremaker knows that a scraper takes a different burr for removing planer marks than for finishing off figured maple.

The majority of turners use the burr off the grinder. However, a cabinet- or furnituremaker's burnisher *(Photo 1)* can pull up a burr. A diamond hone (flat, round, or a slip) will perform the same task.

Many years ago, some turners raised burrs on scrapers with an India slipstone, and it worked. When diamond hones evolved, we found out they raised burrs even easier.

All of these burr types have different applications. The burr off the grinder does not seem to differ radically with the grit of the wheel, but you can vary the amount of pressure applied with the burnisher and hone when raising a burr.

## How to raise a burr

When using the burnisher or a diamond hone, begin at the grinder to raise a burr. Remove the grinder burr by honing the top of the scraper, and then pull a fresh burr with either a burnisher or hone. As the burr wears, hone the top again to remove any evidence of the burr, then pull up a fresh burr. You can usually perform this raising, removing, and raising again three to five times before you must return to the grinder to create a new burr and repeat the sequence.

## Two approaches to wood

Turners use one of two approaches to contact the scraper and wood. The first is what can be called "normal" scraping mode: The blade is flat on the rest, handle in back is slightly elevated, rest at a level to allow only the edge of the tool with *no* bevel to contact the wood *(Photo 2)*. The turning stock is usually contacted at the centerline or slightly above.

In what turners have dubbed "shear scraping," tilt the scraper in the direction of the cut to around 45 to 70 degrees, usually cutting higher (above centerline) on the workpiece and again with no bevel contacting the wood *(Photo 3)*.

## The test

With tools tuned, with different burrs (or even without a burr) and used as described above, the authors wished to determine the nature of the burrs and the wood finishes produced.

For turning stock, we selected kiln-dried yellow poplar (not an easy choice for scraping methods).

The poplar was approached in a challenging way: hollowing end grain. Turning trials used poplar from the same long section of 3×3" stock, the same lathe speed (around 1,000 rpm), and the same size and shape of high-speed steel (HSS) radius scraper (1-1/4" wide and 3/8" thick). After Alan completed the turning trials, he shipped the five scrapers and turned samples to Jerry. Labels did not hint which wood was prepared with which scraper.

## The wood

Although it is known that various sharpening methods produce different edges, does sharpening really affect the way in which the tool cuts?

The poplar end-grain samples were examined at up to 100× under the same imaging microscope (see sidebar). A low-magnification image of the poplar is shown *(Photo 4)*. All magnified images were made with the same grain orientation. In each sample, an area of cross-grain turning was selected because it has the highest probability of tearing.

To illustrate the true underlying grain structure of the poplar, an end-grain face was sanded through a series of papers to 1,000 grit *(Photo 5)*. Note that this image clearly illustrates the beautiful nature of the wood with the reddish intersecting fiber elements and the large population of sectioned white resin-filled vessels or pores. The degree to which this underlying structure is revealed by the tool cutting action is assumed to be a measure of relative edge sharpness.

Based upon the appearance of the cut poplar faces, the sharpest cutting edge was Scraper #5, closely followed by Scraper #4. Each of these tools was polished on the top face prior to raising the burrs. There is a clear improvement between #1 and #2, indicating that polishing of the top of the tool improves the quality of the raised burr.

## Observations

Burrs are tiny! The largest burrs observed were on the order of 0.001" to 0.002" in height. It is amazing how effectively these small edges can cut.

Shear scraping *(Photos 6 and 7)* provides a somewhat better surface than flat scraping, but the effect is small when compared to the effects of edge and top-surface preparation.

The shapes of the burrs are a function of how they are raised and the finish of the top surface on which they are raised.

Simply polishing the top of the tools prior to raising a burr by grinding improves the resulting cut surface dramatically. This also may suggest that a finer grind might also improve burr quality.

*Alan Lacer (AlanLacer.com) is a woodturner, teacher, and writer living near River Falls, WI. Dr. Jerry Wright (jeryl.wright@crucible.com) is a woodturner and vice president of technology for Crucible Specialty Metals in Syracuse, NY. He earned an Sc.D. in metallurgy from Massachusetts Institute of Technology.*

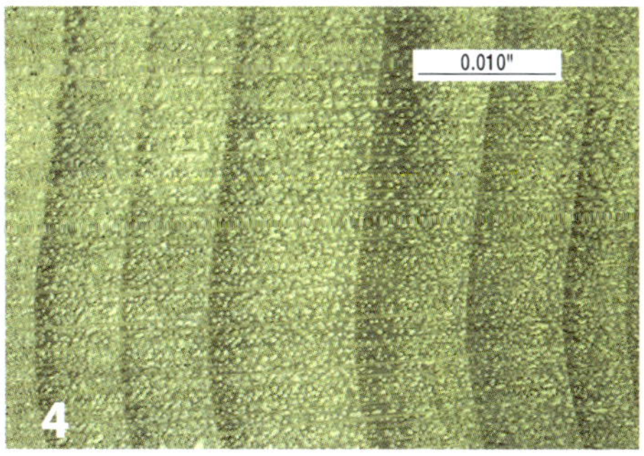


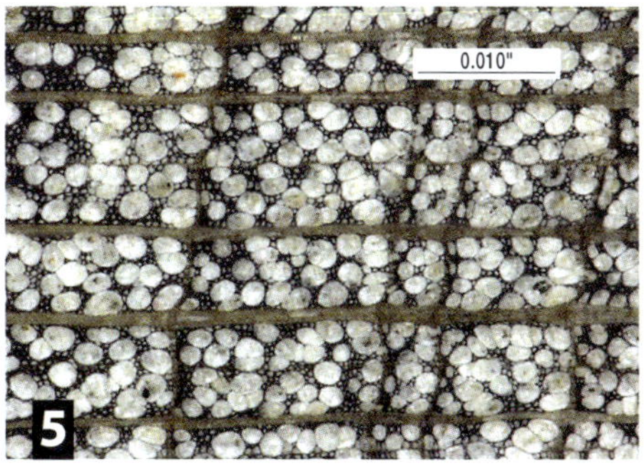

This poplar sample was turned by shear scraping using a tool prepared as Scraper #4 (burr raised by burnishing). White pores are beginning to be resolved. However, the wood fibers are more clearly defined than by scraping alone.

This poplar sample was turned by shear scraping using a tool prepared as Scraper #5 (burr raised with a diamond hone). It contains reasonably resolved white pores and clear structure definition. The wood fibers are somewhat better defined.

## Under the microscope

Woodturners know that their fingers are precise measuring devices. They use them to size vessels and wall thicknesses, and measure the progress made toward a smooth turned or sanded finish. They also use them to determine the sharpness or presence of an edge on turning tools. Our fingers are excellent for feeling the presence or absence of a burr on a scraper. Turners can't see such burrs, but they know they're there!

Much has been written about the many ways to develop the perfect cutting edge, but little has been published to demonstrate what these edges truly look like. One of the reasons for this lack of photographic evidence is the difficulty in producing images with a combination of high magnification and extensive depth of field. Traditionally, this has been accomplished through the use of scanning electron microscopy (SEM). The downside of this approach is that color images cannot be produced and only small samples can be examined.

In the past few years, digital imaging optical microscopes have become available, which not only allow high depth of field color photography, but also allow the computer assimilation of multiple photo "slices" into images with extraordinary depth of field.

The tool edges and corresponding wood surfaces in this study were examined with a 54 megapixel optical imaging microscope. Each edge was photographed at a magnification of 200×. The field of view at this magnification is approximately 3/64" wide. Photos of top views as well as angled views depict the nature of the cutting edge as well as the roles played by the bevel ground surface and the finish of the tool tops.

All scrapers were determined to be type M2 high-speed steel (HSS) and confirmed the manufacturer's labeling as HSS. Scraping was accomplished using two turning methods—flat scraping and shear scraping.

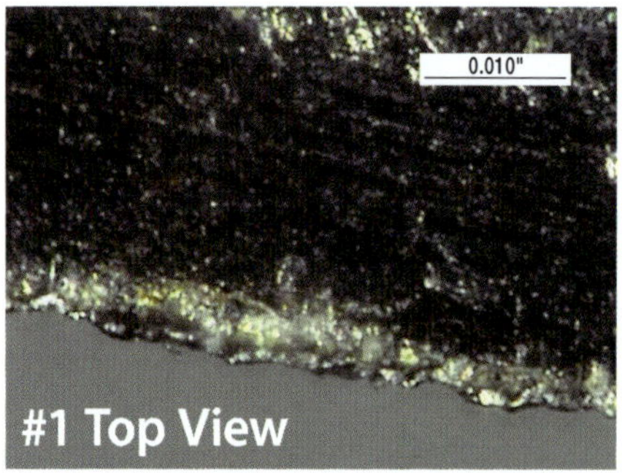

Scraper #1 was prepared by grinding the bevel on a 60-grit wheel. The top of the tool was the ground finish as received from the manufacturer. The burr was produced by the deformation of the tool edge by the force of the wheel surface. The top surface finish appears to have increased the coarseness of the edge. The burr has a stippled appearance. Note that at this magnification, the burr still does not appear sharp.

Poplar sample #1 shows a torn surface. It was turned with the scraper as received from the factory (not polished on top, tool sharpened on a 60-grit wheel). The white pores are nearly obscured and the reddish fibers are barely visible. Fracturing and tearing of the wood matrix is apparent.

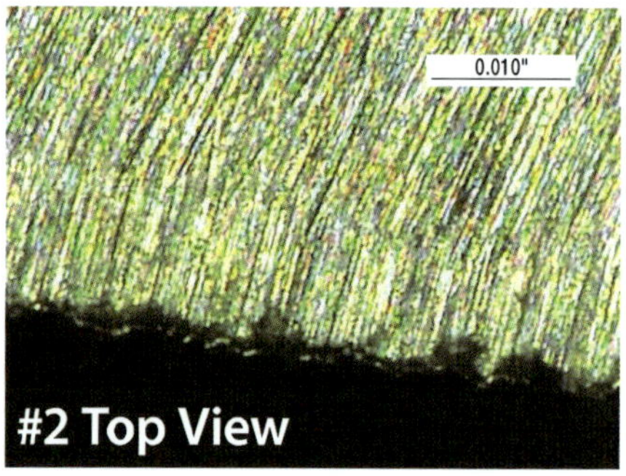

Scraper #2 was prepared in the same manner as #1, except that prior to raising the burr, the top of the tool was polished. Note that this polishing appears to have helped create a finer burr with shorter and more frequent stipples.

Poplar sample #2 was turned with a tool prepared as #1, except that the top was polished prior to grinding. Again, the pores are nearly obscured and there is some evidence of wood tearing.

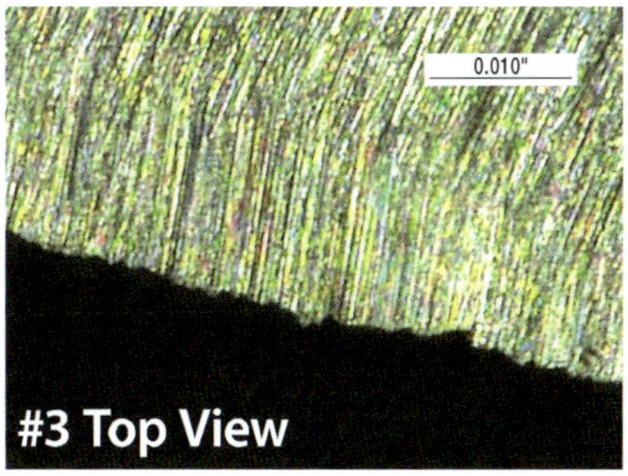


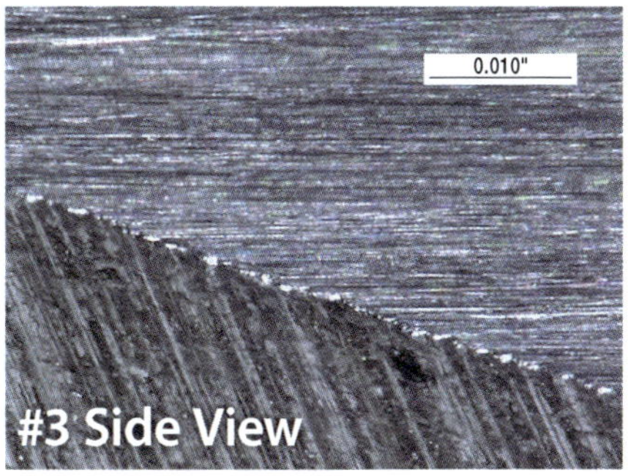

Scraper #3 was prepared as scraper #2, except that the burr was removed by polishing. There is no evidence of a burr and the top view shows the jagged nature of the 60-grit bevel grind. The sharpness of the cutting edge is limited by the intersection of the two surfaces.

Poplar sample #3 was turned with a tool with the burr removed by polishing. The poplar sample illustrates a smeared structure with multiple tears.

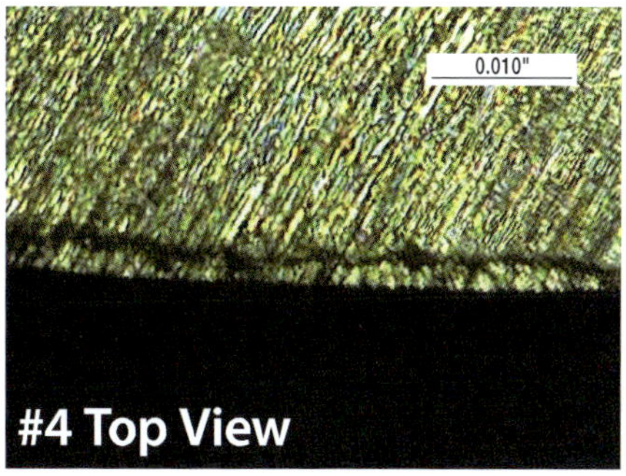

Scraper #4 was prepared in the same manner as #3, and then a burr was raised using a burnisher. The burnisher deforms the edge. The top view of the tool edge indicates that the burnisher raised a continuous burr, which is different in character from the grinding wheel-induced burrs. (The pressure applied during burnishing can control these burrs.) The edge view shows a varying degree of stippling which suggests that this edge is controlled by the top polished surface.

Poplar sample #4, turned with a scraper with a burr that was raised by burnishing, contains white pores that are beginning to be resolved and clear evidence of the reddish fibers.

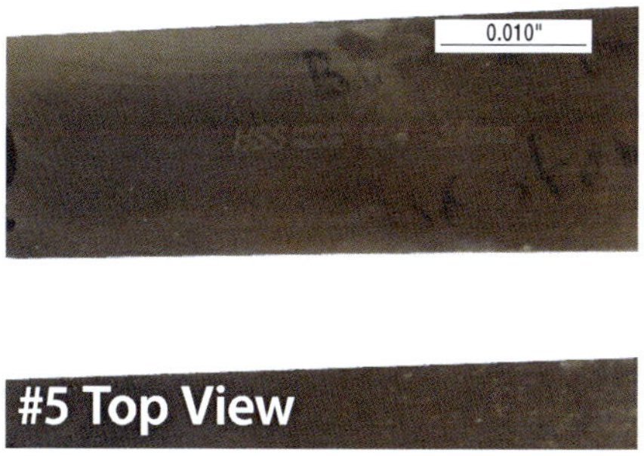


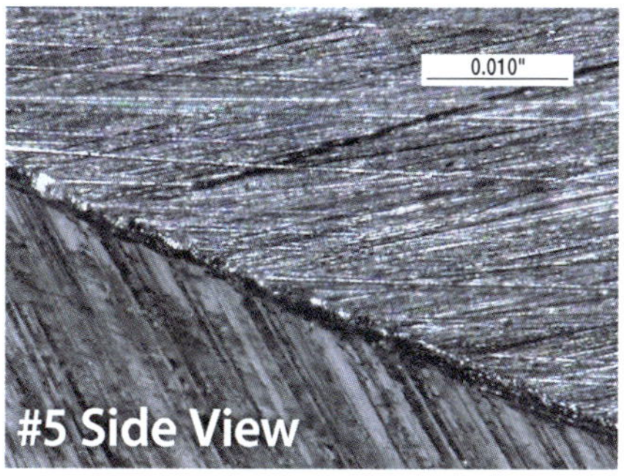


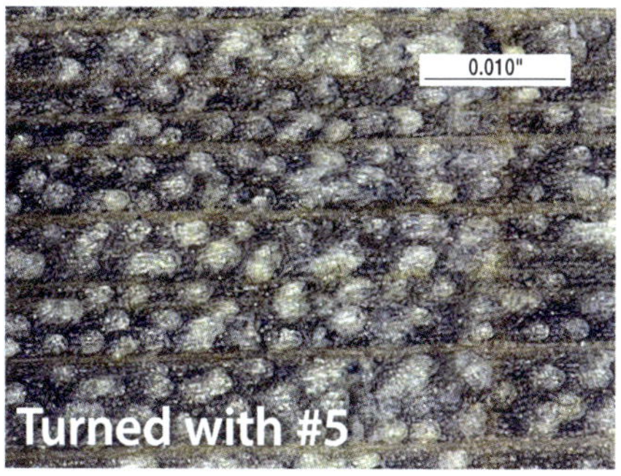


Scraper #5 was prepared in the same manner as #3, and the burr was then formed using a diamond hone. The burr raised is similar to burr #2 and reinforces the concept that the top finish is important in burr formation.

Poplar sample #5 was turned with a tool whose burr was raised with a diamond hone. It shows reasonably resolved white pores, clear structure definition, and no evidence of tearing.

25364300R00041

Printed in Great Britain
by Amazon